WOMEN
PRAY

WOMEN
PRAY

Voices through the Ages,
from Many Faiths,
Cultures, and Traditions

Edited and with introductions by
MONICA FURLONG

Walking Together, Finding the Way
SKYLIGHT PATHS Publishing

Women Pray:
Voices through the Ages, from Many Faiths, Cultures, and Traditions

2002 Second Printing (revised)
2001 First Printing
© 2001 by Monica Furlong

Library of Congress Cataloging-in-Publication Data
Women pray : voices through the ages, from many faiths, cultures, and traditions / edited and with introductions by Monica Furlong.
p.   cm.
ISBN 1-893361-25-X (hardcover)
ISBN 978-1-68336-512-9 (paperback)
1. Women — Prayer-books and devotions — English.
I. Furlong, Monica.
BL625.7.W64   2001
291.4'33'082 — dc21

2001001675

SkyLight Paths Publishing is creating a place where people of different spiritual traditions come together for challenge and inspiration, a place where we can help each other understand the mystery that lies at the heart of our existence.

SkyLight Paths sees both believers and seekers as a community that increasingly transcends traditional boundaries of religion and denomination — people wanting to learn from each other, *walking together, finding the way.*

Manufactured in the United States

SkyLight Paths, "Walking Together, Finding the Way" and colophon are trademarks of LongHill Partners, Inc., registered in the U.S. Patent and Trademark Office.

Walking Together, Finding the Way
Published by SkyLight Paths Publishing
An imprint of Turner Publishing Company
4507 Charlotte Avenue, Suite 100
Nashville, TN 37209
Tel: (615) 255-2665
www.skylightpaths.com

Contents

Introduction

Prayer, to pray, are words that are so much part of our language that we rarely examine the idea and ask what it means. The obvious meaning, the one that a child would probably give if asked to define the word prayer, is "talking to God" or "asking God for something." Many of us, whether we believe in God or not, find ourselves blindly asking for help when our need is great enough—it is an aspect of our helplessness in the face of illness, death, bereavement, and other painful aspects of being human. The idea of talking to God opens up a vista. It beckons us out of a purely human perspective, and invites us to try to see the world, and ourselves within it, from a different angle. "It draws God who is great into a heart which is small" said Mechthild of Magdeburg. It is almost like the experience of the early astronauts, looking at earth from distant space instead of from a position on the earth itself. They found that first external vision astonishing, a source of wonder, and perhaps they experienced an impulse to reassess the human place within a much vaster context.

Mystics of all cultures have been similarly affected by a sense of wonder and vastness as they contemplated the presence of God. It is part of the human condition that we get stuck in our own local perspective. For example, I bring the limitations of my own perspective both to the selection of this material and to my understanding of it. How could it be otherwise? These are the limitations of a white Western Christian. To many from different cultures and from different religions, the emphases would be different. Geographically, nationally, intellectually, and emotionally, our natural tendency seems to be provincial, chauvinistic, lacking in imagination about, and sympathy for, what we do not directly know, though we can and should struggle against this blindness. But our personal experience, our joys, our loves, our worries, our labors, and our sorrows fill our consciousness until our personal concerns can block out all else. The great religions of the world, however, have always reminded us that we need release from that cramped perspective. We need stories, festivals,

Sabbaths, ceremonies, meditations to jolt us out of our pathetic narrowmindedness, our obsession with the internal village street. They remind us that we are bigger than our egos, that we belong to a larger enterprise altogether. And many of those stories, festivals, and ceremonies, though they differ from culture to culture and country to country, have centered on the idea of God.

God has been many things to many people—the sun, the moon, dancing energy, life force, creator, king, judge, lawgiver, father, mother, the earth itself, as well as being manifested in animal form. To the Jews, God has been a transforming presence who gave them a powerful identity and sustained them through centuries of dispersal. To them and to others suffering terrible forms of oppression, God has been a witness at a time when they had no other. To the saints, God has been a lover. The section "Love Unknown" in this collection shows what a poignant experience that has been. To women of our own time, to some of the medieval saints both male and female, and to some native peoples, God has been seen as mother, the source of earth's fertility. In classical Greek culture, the gods were a screen for preoccupations as old as human experience: love, sexual passion, war, art, domestic life, and the pleasures of reason.

Buddhism—on the whole avoiding the concept of God, though some Buddhists do retain it—is concerned with a somewhat different method of freeing its followers from their imprisonment in the "passing show" or "the chatter in the skull." The discipline of meditation can take many forms, but like the God-concept it helps to bring about a freeing, slow or immediate, to which the name *enlightenment* is usually given.

Prayer, then, which may take the form of meditation as well as the simpler forms of asking, or thanksgiving, or praying for others, is about a shift of consciousness, or at least an attempt at a shift of consciousness, to a new perspective. If we are less preoccupied with ourselves we are less likely to see others as competitive egos or deadly rivals. Many religions suggest that in some sense we *are* one another. The Anglican poet John Donne famously said that we are not islands—"No man is an island"—but all human beings are "part of the main." Rabbi Shmelke of Nikolsberg said that to strike another human being is like striking ourselves—it is bound to cause us suffering.

Prayer *for* other human beings involves us in their well-being, their health and happiness, and religion has often encouraged its adherents to carry their prayer forward into practical concern—to feed the hungry and house the homeless. Late in the twentieth century and on into the twenty-first, many have started praying also for the earth and its creatures, as the threat to *its* health and survival has become ever plainer. Tribal peoples have usually had an acute awareness of the welfare of the natural world, since their survival depended very directly on the animals and plants that they hunted and gathered. In more "sophisticated" and industrialized cultures, where for generations townspeople have had little to do with the growing or gathering of food, this knowledge is returning only slowly. Some of these prayers indicate a deep, and sometimes tragic, concern for human carelessness about nature. If people need to be cherished, healed, and sustained, then so does the natural world, Westerners are painfully learning. Having lost the old awe and wonder in the face of nature, modern civilizations have plundered the earth, destroying habitats, poisoning waters, hunting or fishing creatures to extinction. The only way back from this desperate situation is a new perspective, a collective turning away from the ego and its greed that all religions have taught.

So prayer is about a new perspective on the world about us, or perhaps the recovery of an earlier perspective. It is about a rediscovery of awe and wonder, of love and joy, of a transforming of grief and pain and loss, of a turning to one another and to the world in which we find ourselves. All this is its territory.

AN ATTITUDE OF MIND

You will notice that not all the contributions to this book are in the traditional forms that we associate with prayer—some are poems, some pieces of prose. Some are songs delighting in the earth and the pleasure of living upon it, some explore relationship with God, some are about daily life, others are about the huge adventures of birth and death. Some freely express joy, others grief. A few are very angry. All of them, however, without exception, are in my view about the perspective that prayer gives. As I made the collection I realized how blurred, at least in my mind, was the distinction between what is a prayer and what is not. It is not necessarily a piece of prose that begins by addressing God directly—in fact, some pieces of writing that do this feel anything but prayerful. A prayer, I came to feel, is always about an attitude of mind that lifts experience out of a narrow context and perceives the beauty, and sometimes the terror, with which all our lives are shot through. Some inkling of awe is perhaps the common ingredient. I invite you to approach these selections without expectations, as a way of discovering the attitude of prayer in both traditional and very unexpected places.

THE VOICE OF THE SILENT

And women's prayers? What is it about women's prayers that make them need a book to themselves? Are women's voices so different from men's?

It is the unanswerability of that last question that explains the need for a book like this.

For it is only in the last twenty to thirty years (a very short time in the long span of human culture) that women's voices have been raised—at least in large numbers—in public prayer.

In most religious cultures throughout history, for a complex variety of reasons, women have been silent. In Christianity, the advice of St. Paul to the Corinthian congregation in the middle of the first century—that "women should be silent in the churches"—was observed with an unquestioning precision so that up until the 1960s, and much later in some cases, women did not preach in churches, or, often enough, read or sing in choirs. (There were exceptions to this. The Shakers were led by a woman, Ann Lee; the early Methodists allowed women to speak in public and to take services; and the Society of Friends has always allowed an exceptional role to women.) The enforced silence of women was especially tragic, since increasing evidence shows that it was not like that at the beginning of Christianity. Women played a key part in establishing the early Christian churches and, as the story of Perpetua reveals, were prepared to suffer as martyrs alongside the men and to be vocal about their reasons. But as so often happens, a sense of propriety killed the early liberation; the early churches, eager to acquire adherents, worried about "what people might think."

In Judaism, too—from which, of course, the Christians borrowed extensively—women had a very limited public role, partly because, as in so many older cultures, women seemed somehow subsumed in the family as daughter, wife, or widow. Scholars point out how often women in ancient scriptures are not named—even poor Jephtha's daughter, required to give up her life for her people, is not allowed an individual identity beyond being her father's child.

It is not easy for us now to get into the mind-set that saw women simply as adjuncts of men—one that very often deprived women of education and denied many of their gifts. But I do not think it helps for modern women to view the past as a kind of male conspiracy to keep women down, because the blindness around the assumptions were so universal, among women as well as men, that almost no one, women or men, saw through them before the Enlightenment brought them into question. Perhaps this was because women were so demonstrably constrained by the huge burden of childbearing. Until very recent times it was common for married women to give birth as many as ten times, and even if they survived the constant experience of pregnancy and childbirth (and many did not), that, and the laborious running of a home, left them little time for a public role. Nor were unmarried women notably freer, except in remote instances where they owned private wealth. The life of Christina Rossetti shows the domestic labor that was expected of a daughter, even if, as in Christina's case, she was more gifted than her brother—from whom, of course, no domestic labor was expected.

There *were* women who survived or overcame their multiple handicaps—Christina Rossetti is one of them—and wrote prayers and poems that achieved publication, but many must have been lost, since women's writing was not prized, and many women lacked the contacts enjoyed by Christina in her search for a publisher.

Christina is part of the long procession of women, a kind of underground stream, who from early in history had tried to express themselves in writing, very often on religious themes, but whose work only broke surface very occasionally.

EARLY WRITING BY WOMEN

Among the earliest prayers and poems by women that we have are those of Sappho. They are fragments of astonishing beauty and simplicity; religion and secular concerns are meshed together, as in so much early writing. The next rising of the spring was not until the Middle Ages, hundreds of years later, when a formidable group of religious women began to express themselves in prose and poetry. It is not surprising that quite a lot of this writing emerged either from convents, or from convent-educated women. Convents, which often had excellent libraries, were among the few places where women could obtain a good education, and nuns were some of the few women who had the leisure as well as the skills to be able to read. Heloise and Beatrijs of Nazareth were, because of convent education, able to read and write in Latin. Hildegard of Bingen, who was brought up by her hermit aunt from the age of about eight, was painfully aware that her Latin was not good. Many medieval women could not read and write at all, while some could read but not write (the more difficult skill of the two). The fourteenth-century Margery Kempe, the mother of fourteen children, minded bitterly that she could not read and write, and was obliged to employ an amanuensis to write down her religious thoughts.

Most of those who could read and write were unlike Heloise or Hildegard in knowing Latin, and could only write in the vernacular: the local dialect of their country. This excluded them from public religious discourse, which traditionally took place in Latin. Suddenly, however, in the early medieval period, there was a kind of democratic movement in the world of religion — an uprush of writing in the vernacular by men as well as women — and many women were at last liberated to write. Angela of Foligno, Hadewijch of Brabrant, Mechthild of Magdeburg, Catherine of Siena, Beatrijs of Nazareth (who chose the Flemish dialect as her medium although she was a Latin scholar), and perhaps the most important, Julian of Norwich, were among them, to our lasting gain. The Beguines, the lay movement for women in Northern Europe, which included as members women who lived alone and others who lived together in small communities, not only performed good works among the poor, but also ran schools and probably taught adults to read and write. The Beguines produced many distinguished writers.

Many of these women writers were widely read across Europe, by men as well as women, perhaps because they often wrote powerfully about their experiences rather than expounding arguments and doctrines. One of the Beguines, Marguerite Porete, wrote a book so influential that it got her burned by the Inquisition, and in the wake of this disaster one or two Beguines joined more conventional religious orders, probably as a form of protection. What is remarkable—what perhaps clinched the women's literary success—was both the personal note with which they often wrote, as well as the passion with which they wrote of their love for God.

At about the same time, in other parts of the world, other women—a very few—were also emerging from obscurity, the Sufi mystic Rabi'a and the Hindu mystic Mirabai among them. The religious passion that they express is interestingly similar to that of their European counterparts.

Women's religious and other writing then went underground again, though there were moments when it reappeared with distinction—in particular in the work of Teresa of Ávila.

THE MODERN ERA

In the nineteenth century, Western women were slowly beginning to formulate their resentment at exclusion from the field of religion (and, of course, from other areas), putting down roots of dissent that were to flower in the twentieth century. The American Elizabeth Cady Stanton criticized the way in which the Bible was used to keep women subordinate. In England, the attempt to forbid women to stand as candidates for the new lay church councils in England brought about what a historian calls "the first clear statement of Christian feminism." There was a flowering of women's religious writing, particularly as far as hymn writing was concerned. Anna Laetitia Waring, Cecil Frances Alexander, Frances Ridley Havergal, Maria Willis, and Christina Rossetti herself all wrote excellent hymns that generations of Christians have sung, and I was delighted to include some of them in this book. If we find in them what, for the modern woman's taste, seems an excessive emphasis on self-surrender, on the speaker's extreme sinfulness and general unworthiness, nevertheless the passion of the work and the skill of the writing still make them very appealing—an important milestone on women's long journey to be treated as fully equal and human.

But the acceptance of women as full participants on the religious scene had a long journey ahead of it and is still not complete. Examining books of prayers edited by male clergy as late as the 1960s and 1970s, it is still possible to find women's voices almost entirely absent, as if none of the great medieval writers or the nineteenth-century hymn writers had existed.

But change was coming, and coming fast. It came partly because, throughout the twentieth century, women were becoming emancipated, moving from obtaining the franchise to full secondary and tertiary education, and thence to professional status, economic parity, control of their fertility, and the other changes we now, in the West, take for granted. One of the results of this was that women at last had the confidence to contest their lowly status in church and synagogue. Spreading through Presbyterian, Baptist, and Methodist churches was a demand that women should be ordained as ministers, and this was taken up by Episcopal churches in the United States, Britain, and other parts of the world. This change did not come easily, at least in the Episcopal churches, and as the struggle continued, women, and sometimes women and men together, banded into prayer groups, house churches, and small movements designed to advance women's ministry.

This produced a flowering of liturgy, written not by clergy but by ordinary worshipers who wanted religious services to express *their* concerns, and who were exasperated at the way language of the "Dearly beloved brethren" type had excluded women.

Judaism too moved to ordain women as rabbis, though in Judaism as in Christianity, the more conservative groups felt unable to support such a change. In Judaism too there was a flowering of women's prayers. At about the same time, Western Buddhism also began to offer women more leadership roles. But perhaps in all religions there have always been some women, like the Hindu Mirabai, who broke the mold, though word of them has not always been preserved.

Moving toward a new sense of identity in religions that had kept them silent and subordinate, Christian and Jewish women alike had to struggle with scriptures in which women were excluded from much of the action. For this reason, certain passages of the Bible—the song of Miriam, the story of Ruth and Naomi (a very moving account of solidarity between women), and the Wisdom literature in which wisdom, an aspect of God, is given a feminine persona—all became very important to women urging change. Christians relished these passages as well as the significance of the fact—often obscured in liturgy and teaching—that it was a woman, Mary Magdalene, who made the first momentous announcement of the Resurrection.

The new thinking about women produced predictable upheavals. Many women in synagogues and churches, who had unthinkingly gone along with their silent and lowly status in the past, began to raise difficult questions. (Other women, it must be said, were equally indignant that the issues had been raised at all.) Some left institutional religion for small prayer groups or for religious bodies like the Quakers, whose attitudes to women had been more exemplary. Many left organized religion altogether. Others sought religious expression by seeking out ancient forms of worship from far-distant periods of history, when, supposedly, matriarchy had ruled. But something significant had happened. Women were no longer prepared to be silent in churches and synagogues. They had found their voices after the centuries of suppression, and discovered that they were strong and often lyrical. Just as, in singing, women's voices complement men's voices in choirs, so in their perceptions, their understanding, and their particular wisdoms they could add something of value to religious discourse. It is not, probably, that women are so very different from men — it is rather that their life experience often has been, and still is, a very different one.

So are women's prayers turning out to be significantly different from men's prayers? It is perhaps too soon to know, though this collection of prayers and poems may go a little way to suggest a conclusion.

FINDING OUR ROOTS

One striking feature is that modern women's prayers and perspective are often taken up with "roots," with reestablishing a partially lost identity, as well as self-esteem, as they seek to restore some of what has been suppressed and to put themselves in a landscape in which there is continuity with a female past that has been largely obliterated: the generations of women who had no names, could not read or write, and were excluded from public discourse.

Many contemporary women's prayers also are very taken up with themes of justice and of poverty (injustice and poverty have affected the lives of a good many women, though men too suffer in this regard, of course). Ecological issues too come up a good deal, in my experience, in prayer groups. Whether women worry or care more about these issues than men, I would not like to say. Movingly, in Oodgeroo of the Noonuccal's poem "We Are Going," the destruction of the earth and its creatures is linked to the destruction of Australian Aboriginal communities.

Bearing children and caring for them were issues rarely thought to be of much spiritual interest before women began to write out of their experiences of childbirth. Until modern times, men often had little to do with either and were unlikely to pray about it, except, sometimes with desperation, that their wives might survive the ordeal. There is less writing on the subject by women than you might expect, considering its huge importance in many women's lives. Perhaps women still need to convince themselves that issues that primarily affect them have spiritual depth.

One of the things I have enjoyed most about compiling this collection has been the ability to draw from a pool of women's writing that covers a huge span of history. It is wonderful to get a glimpse of women's ceremonies in ancient Greece—ceremonies that were about Aphrodite, Hestia, or the moon. It is moving to contemplate the religious passion of the Sufi Rabi'a or the Hindu *bhakta* Mirabai, whose words and feelings are strikingly similar to those of their medieval Christian contemporaries. I love the metrical mastery of the nineteenth-century women hymn writers, and if there are undertones of masochism here and there in their work, it echoes the way women have dealt for centuries with powerlessness, a kind of "making the best of a bad job." The amazing voice of forgiveness from a concentration camp, and Irina Ratushinskaya's clear, moral voice from a KGB prison, are wonderful evocations of goodness and love in situations where it seems unimaginable that both would not be destroyed. And I also found a sense of hope in the fact that many distinguished contemporary women poets—Denise Levertov, Judith Wright—have such a profound sense of the wonder and awe of human existence and of the natural world.

It has been good, too, to look at life through the window of different religious viewpoints: Buddhism, Judaism, Christianity, Native American spirituality, and others. I enjoyed the Buddhist insistence on "getting free," the ritual grace of both Judaism and Christianity, the ecstatic Native American delight in the world of trees and mountains and creatures. I liked the humor, conscious and unconscious, of one or two of the pieces: of the little girl who asked God to try to be fair to girls even though he was male himself, and, more darkly, Betsy Sholl sternly asking God, in the persona of Job's wife, what he thought he was up to in disposing of *her* ten children just to teach Job a lesson.

Virtually every poem or prayer in the book has been written by a woman, but there are one or two important exceptions. In describing Simone Weil's profound religious experience brought on by reading George Herbert's poem "Love," I have quoted Herbert's poem in full so the reader may recall the words that so profoundly moved Simone Weil. Since Homer is wonderful at describing women's ceremonies, of which otherwise we know little, I have used some of his descriptions, beautifully translated by Charles Boer.

THE VOICE OF "ANONYMOUS"

More controversially, I have used some anonymous pieces of writing: one from Africa, others by American Indians, and some from Gaelic-speaking Scotland. Attributing songs and poems to individuals is a relatively late phenomenon, and in cultures that still do not attribute authorship, it is usually the case that some at least are written, or anyhow spoken, by women. So rather than exclude such material altogether, it seemed better to include material that concerned itself with what had traditionally been women's concerns, such as children and cleaning house. One or two prayers, particularly in the first section, cannot even be said to have this shaky justification, but they have such a joyful sense of the wonder of life that I have included them anyway. Some of them were probably written by women, and if the others were not, I am using the excuse that for centuries women were obliged to hide behind "anonymous," and now I am shamelessly claiming some "anonymous" territory back on their behalf.

This book has a practical purpose. The prayers and poems are intended not only to be read at home, as one reads any other book, but also to be used in the quiet of prayer groups or in the public discourse of worshiping communities—indeed, wherever such insights are valued and used. It is for those who love God, or wish they did; for those who love humanity, and wish they loved it better; and those who love the natural world, but feel at a loss to halt its damage and decline. Prayer may spur us to better and wiser efforts.

Finally, I would like to make two personal acknowledgments: to the St. Hilda Community of London, a prayer group of women and men that has worked for fourteen years to bring about a new attitude to women in the Christian churches. I have loved being a member, and I owe them a debt of gratitude, love and laughter for some marvelous evenings spent in their company. And I would also like to thank David O'Neal, my editor at SkyLight Paths, whose idea the book was. I have very much valued his appreciation and encouragement, and his many good suggestions and helpful comments.

MONICA FURLONG
London

1

EARTH OUR MOTHER

Joy and gratitude for the natural world can unite writers from a wide variety of different cultural backgrounds and religions. It is something all human beings have in common—the experience of the earth they share and upon which they depend for their existence. Tribal peoples say this more unselfconsciously than the rest of us; like the writer of the Navajo chant, they know themselves to be part of what they describe.

Earth, our mother, breathe forth life
all night sleeping
now awaking
in the east
now see the dawn

Earth, our mother, breathe and waken
leaves are stirring
all things moving
new day coming
life renewing

Eagle soaring, see the morning
see the new mysterious morning
something marvelous and sacred
though it happens every day
Dawn the child of God and Darkness.

Pawnee prayer

For all things bright and beautiful,
For all things dark and mysterious and lovely,
For all things green and growing and strong,
For all things weak and struggling to push life up
    through rocky earth,
For all human faces, hearts, minds, and hands
    which surround us,
And for all nonhuman minds and hearts, paws
    and claws, fins and wings,
For this Life and the life of this world,
For all that you have laid before us, O God,
We lay our thankful hearts before you.

Gail A. Riccuiti

The mountains, I become part of it . . .
The herbs, the fir tree, I become part of it.
The morning mists, the clouds, the gathering
    waters,
I become part of it.
The wilderness, the dew drops, the pollen . . .
I become part of it.

Navajo chant

Birds nest in my arms,
on my shoulders, behind my knees,
between my breasts there are quails,
they must think I'm a tree.
The swans think I'm a fountain,
they all come down and drink when I talk.
When sheep pass, they pass over me,
and perched on my fingers, the sparrows eat,
the ants think I'm the earth,
and men think I'm nothing.

Gloria Fuertes

O beautiful for spacious skies,
For amber waves of grain,
For purple mountains' majesty,
Above the fruited plain.
America, America,
God shed his grace on thee,
And crown thy good with brotherhood
From sea to shining sea.

Katharine Lee Bates

I believe God is everything. . . . Everything that is or ever was or ever will be. And when you can feel that, and be happy to feel that, you've found It. . . . My first step from the old white man was the trees. Then air. Then birds. Then other people. But one day when I was sitting quiet and feeling like a motherless child, which I was, it come to me: that feeling of being part of everything, not separate at all. I knew that if I cut a tree, my arm would bleed. And I laughed and I cried and I run all round the house. I knew just what it was. In fact, when it happen, you can't miss it.

Alice Walker, The Color Purple

This is what I want to happen: that our earth
    mother
may be clothed in ground corn four times over,
that frost flowers cover her over entirely,
that the mountain pines far away over there
may stand close to each other in the cold,
that the weight of snow crack some branches!
In order that the country may be this way
I have made my prayer sticks into something
    alive.

Zuni prayer

THE NEW MOON

She of my love is the new moon,
The King of all creatures blessing her;
Be mine a good purpose
Towards each creature of creation.

Holy be each thing
Which she illumines;
Kindly be each deed
Which she reveals.

Be her guidance on land
With all beset ones;
Be her guidance on the sea
With all distressed ones.

May the moon of moons
Be coming through thick clouds
On me and on every mortal
Who is coming through affliction.

May the virgin of my love
Be coming through dense dark clouds
To me and to each one
Who is in tribulation.

May the King of grace
Be helping my hand
Now and for ever
Till my resurrection day.

Gaelic, Anonymous

Father our Creator,
You created all things, seen and unseen,
Listen to my silent prayer as I stand before you.

As my weary eyes look back over distant
    horizons,
Back to those days where my people walked,
The foot prints of my grandfathers are imprinted
    on the earth
And their images become real to me.

I see my Grandfathers standing tall and strong,
warriors of long ago
I hear them singing
I hear them dancing
And my spirit moves within me.

They told me of the emus fighting
And the kangaroos picking up the scent of our
    hunters
The images fade away as I feel the hurt of my
    people.

I can hear the cries of my Grandmothers as
    they cry
for their children.

Grandfather, you can see me as I stand here and
    feel this hurt.
Father, Creator, is this the purpose of my being
    here
Or is it your plan to reshape my people
To be once again the proud race it once was?

Let me walk with you and my Grandfathers
Towards the dawning of a proud and new nation.
I thank you for my Sacred Being.
Amen.

Aboriginal Jubilee Prayer

2

THE VALLEY OF LOVE
AND DELIGHT

This section is about the joy of being human — the sheer pleasure of being alive, the wonder of loving another human being or of loving God. These experiences are often seen as separate from one another. I do not believe that the mystics quoted here believe that to be the case. For them, all love is inseparable, although it finds its purpose and fulfilment in God. To quote Beatrijs of Nazareth, "she feels her spirit roams free through the depths and the heights and the immensity of love."

'Tis the gift to be simple, 'tis the gift to be free,
'Tis the gift to come down where you ought to be
And when you find yourself in the place just right
'Twill be in the valley of love and delight.

Shaker song

May it be delightful my house,
From my head may it be delightful,
To my feet may it be delightful,
Where I lie may it be delightful,
All above me may it be delightful,
All around me may it be delightful.

Navajo chant

YERUSHALAYIM SHEL ZAHAV

The mountain air is as clear as wine, and the
    smell of the pine tree
is carried on the evening breeze with the sound
    of bells.
The city is imprisoned in a sleep of tree and
    stone,
the city which dwells alone and in its heart
    a wall.
Jerusalem of gold, of copper and of light,
I am a harp for all your songs.

We have returned to the water cisterns, to the
    market and the squares.
A *shofar* is heard on the Temple Mount in the
    Old City.
In the caves in the rocks a thousand windows
    gleam.
Let us once again descend to the Dead Sea by
    way of Jericho.

Jerusalem of gold, of copper and of light,
I am a harp for all your songs.

But when I come today to sing to you and to
    crown you,
I am less than the least of your children and the
    last of your poets,
for your name burns the lips like the kiss of a
    seraph.
If I forget you, O Jerusalem, which is all gold.
Jerusalem of gold, of copper and of light,
I am a harp for all your songs.

Naomi Shemer

THE SOUL IN LOVE

And so as the fish swims in the vastness of the oceans and rests in the deeps, and as the bird boldly soars in the heights and the vastness of the air, in the same way she feels her spirit roam free through the depths and the heights and the immensity of love.

Beatrijs of Nazareth

THE BIRTHDAY

My heart is like a singing bird
Whose nest is in a water'd shoot;
My heart is like an apple-tree
Whose boughs are bent with thick-set fruit;
My heart is like a rainbow shell
That paddles in a halcyon sea;
My heart is gladder than all these,
Because my love is come to me.

Raise me a dais of silk and down;
Hang it with vair and purple dyes;
Carve it in doves and pomegranates,
And peacocks with a hundred eyes;
Work it in gold and silver grapes,
In leaves and silver fleurs-de-lys;
Because the birthday of my life
Is come, my love is come to me.

Christina Rossetti

BLISS

My beloved came,
I watched the road,
and I, the solitary,
attained Him.

I decorated the plate
for *puja,*
I gave my jewels
to Him.

And finally,
He sent messages,
He came.

Bliss adorns me,
Hari is a sea
of love.

My eyes are linked
to his,
in Love,

Mira, a sea of bliss,
admits
the Dark-one.

Mirabai

Puja is an offering in worship; the "Dark-one" is the god
Krishna.

THE VISITING SEA

As the inhastening tide doth roll,
Home from the deep, along the whole
    Wide shining strand, and floods the caves,
    —Your love comes filling with happy waves
The open sea-shore of my soul.

But inland from the seaward spaces,
None knows, not even you, the places
    Brimmed, at your coming, out of sight
    —The little solitudes of delight
This tide constrains in dim embraces.

You see the happy shore, wave-rimmed,
But know not of the quiet dimmed
    Rivers your coming floods and fills,
    The little pools 'mid happier hills,
My silent rivulets, over-brimmed.

What! I have secrets from you? Yes.
But, visiting Sea, your love doth press
    And reach in further than you know
    And fills all these, and, when you go,
There's loneliness in loneliness.

Alice Meynell

Nada te turbe,
nada te espante.
Quien a Dios tiene
nada le falta.
Nada te turbe,
nade te espante.
Solo Dios basta.

No need for fear
Or deep despair
Seekers of God
Receive his care.
No need for fear
Or deep despair
We are at home
And God is there.

Prayer of St. Teresa of Ávila

In this good world
The sun burns on puddles
Clouds mass in the sky above the cooling-towers
Snow lies on slag heaps
And detergent floats on rivers limpid as silk.
In this good world
Praise bursts from our lips
Like diamonds
Like jewels from the kind princess's mouth.
In this good world
Our curses turn to praise
Perversity perverted;
Even on the rack
We're held by joy.

Monica Furlong

I am the rose of Sharon, and the lily of the valleys.

As the lily among thorns, so is my love among the daughters.

As the apple tree among the trees of the wood, so is my beloved among the sons.

I sat down under his shadow with great delight, and his fruit was sweet to my taste.

He brought me to the banqueting house, and his banner over me was love.

Stay me with flagons, comfort me with apples, for I am sick of love.

His left hand is under my head, and his right hand doth embrace me.

I charge you, O ye daughters of Jerusalem, by the roes, and by the hinds of the field, that ye stir not up, nor awake my love, till he please.

The voice of my beloved! Behold, he cometh leaping upon the mountains, skipping upon the hills.

My beloved is like a roe or a young hart; behold, he standeth behind our wall, he looketh forth at the windows, shewing himself through the lattice.

My beloved spake, and said unto me, Rise up, my
love, my fair one, and come away.

For, lo, the winter is past, the rain is over and
gone;

The flowers appear on the earth; the time of the
singing of birds is come, and the voice of the
turtle is heard in our land.

The fig putteth forth her green figs, and the vines
with the tender grape give a good smell.
Arise, my love, my fair one, and come away.

My dove, that art in the clefts of the rock, in the
secret places of the stairs, let me see thy
countenance, let me hear thy voice; for sweet
is thy voice, and thy countenance is comely.

Take us the foxes, the little foxes, that spoil the
vines: for our vines have tender grapes.

My beloved is mine, and I am his: he feedeth
among the lilies.

Until the day break, and the shadows flee away,
turn, my beloved, and be thou like a roe or a
young hart upon the mountains.

Song of Solomon 2:1–17

Love penetrates the senses and storms the soul with all its power. When love grows in the soul, then it rises up with great longing to God and flowingly expands to receive the miracle that breaks in upon it. Love melts through the soul and into the senses. And so the body too gains its part and conforms in all ways to love.

Mechthild of Magdeburg

And God said to the soul:
I desired you before the world began.
I desire you now
As you desire me.
And where the desires of two come together
There love is perfected.

Lord, you are my lover,
My longing,
My flowing stream,
My sun,
And I am your reflection.

It is a rare
And a high way,
Which the soul follows,
Drawing the senses after,
Just as the person with sight leads the blind.
In this way the soul is free
And lives without the heart's grief,
Desiring nothing but her Lord,
Who works all things well.

Mechthild of Magdeburg

I learned that love was our Lord's meaning.
And I saw for certain, both here and elsewhere,
that before he ever made us, God loved us;
and that his love has never slackened,
    nor ever shall.
In this love all his works have been done,
and in this love he has made everything serve us;
and in this love our life is everlasting.
Our beginning was when we were made,
but the love in which he made us
    never had beginning.
In this we have our beginning.
All this we shall see in God for ever.
May Jesus grant this.

Julian of Norwich

O to continue to drink deep of the streams of the great salvation, until I wholly lose the thirst for the passing things of earth; to live watching for my Lord, to be wide awake when he comes, to open to him quickly and enjoy his likeness to the full.

Ann Griffiths

3

LOVE UNKNOWN

If the last section described the joy of love, this one describes its more baffling aspects: the searching, the uncertainty, the fear of loss, as evident in some of these mystical writers as in the writers of courtly love by whom many of them were influenced. There is pain — "burning," as Hildegard calls it — in love, though this may be part of our growth into understanding. For the religious writer, it is part of trust, the coming to rely upon God even in moments of darkness. "He knows the way he taketh" says the nineteenth-century Anna Laetitia Waring, and "I will walk with him." Rabi'a is ready to accept what God gives her, even if it is the loss of God himself. What matters, says Hadewijch, is to "commit all your being to love."

Love unknown. Why, why, why?

Angela di Foligno

I slept for a moment,
the Beloved appeared,
when I rose to greet him,
he was
gone.

Some lose him
sleeping,
I lost him,
awake,

Mira's lord, *Girðhara,*
brings happiness to
the
home.

Mirabai

Girðhara means "immovable mountain."

ANTIPHON FOR GOD THE FATHER

Burn, everlasting one, in love
as you loved when you first were
father in the burning
dawn before the world's day!

Loving your son you loved
us all into being; let us
all be his limbs.

See the need that befalls us!
Lift it away from us
and for your child's sake lead us
into safety, into bliss.

Hildegard of Bingen

God! If I worship Thee in fear of Hell, burn me in Hell; and if I worship Thee in hope of Paradise, exclude me from Paradise; but if I worship Thee for Thine own sake, withhold not Thine everlasting beauty.

My Lord, whatever share of this world Thou dost bestow on me, bestow it on Thine enemies, and whatever share of the next world Thou dost give to me, give it to Thy friends— Thou art enough for me.

Rabi'a the Mystic

Like a silkworm weaving
her house with love
from her marrow,

and dying
in her body's threads
winding tight, round
and round.

I burn
desiring what the heart desires.

Cut through, O Lord,
my heart's greed,
and show me
your way out,
lord white as jasmine.

Mahadeviyakka

Passionate, with longing in my eyes,
Searching wide, and seeking nights and days,
Lo! I beheld the Truthful One, the Wise,
Here in my own house to fill my gaze.

Just for a moment a flower grows,
Bright and brilliant on a green-clad tree
Just for a moment a cold wind blows
Through the bare thorns of a thicket free.

Lalleswari, or Lal Diddi, of Kashmir

O love, set your whole mind
On God's love who made you.
Commit all your being to love;
And then you shall heal all your wounds,
Neither fearing pain nor
Fleeing from sorrow in anything.
You should rely on love
And then you shall know what to love and what
    to hate.
Be content with all things:
For that is the sign of love's presence,
And that you are so easily oppressed
Denies you many a beautiful gift.
If you love you wish to trust yourself in God
And keep yourself in charity
Then all shall be yours:
And you shall win your love.

Hadewijch of Brabant

And he showed me more, a little thing, the size of a hazel-nut, on the palm of my hand, round like a ball. I looked at it thoughtfully and wondered 'What is this?' And the answer came, 'It is all that is made.' I marvelled that it continued to exist and did not suddenly disintegrate; it was so small. And again my mind supplied the answer, 'It exists, both now and for ever, because God loves it.' In short, everything owes its existence to the love of God.

Julian of Norwich

In heav'nly love abiding,
no change my heart shall fear;
and safe is such confiding,
for nothing changes here.
The storm may roar without me,
my heart may low be laid,
but God is round about me,
and can I be dismayed?

Wherever he may guide me,
no want shall turn me back;
my Shepherd is beside me,
and nothing can I lack.
His wisdom ever waketh,
his sight is never dim,
he knows the way he taketh,
and I will walk with him.

Green pastures are before me,
which yet I have not seen;
bright skies will soon be o'er me,

where the dark clouds have been.
My hope I cannot measure,
my path to life is free,
my Saviour has my treasure,
and he will walk with me.

Anna Laetitia Waring

Lord, I rack my brains to find ways of loving you and I don't succeed.

Lord, I am here before You like the dry ground upon which the prophet called down the dew.

Lord, I have loved You so long, but don't know how to love You.

Most tender Lord, give me Your arms. I am returning to our home with the tiny steps of a small child.

Gabrielle Bossis

God, the night has passed and the day has dawned. How I long to know if Thou hast accepted my prayers or if Thou hast rejected them. Therefore console me, for it is Thine to console this state of mine. Thou hast given me life and cared for me, and Thine is the glory. If Thou wantst to drive me from Thy door, yet I would not forsake it, for the love that I bear in my heart towards Thee.

Rabi'a the Mystic

Under vaults of cathedrals eternal,
Barefoot where dusty roads wind,
With nakedly trembling candles
People seek a God who is kind.

That He'll understand and take pity
Through the murders, the raving and lies,
That He'll put his hands on temples
As on cruel injuries.

That He'll see the shouting faces,
Dark of souls, eyes that light never knew,
That the fool and the whore He will pardon,
And the priest, and the poet, too.

That He'll save the fleer from pursuers,
That He'll give to the hungry bread . . .
Perhaps God is a cross in a hand's palm?
Perhaps God is a sky as dark as lead?

The road to Him, how discover?
With what measure the hope, pain and grief?
People seek God, a kind one.
God grant they may find and believe.

Irina Ratushinskaya, Odessa, 1970

In 1938 I spent ten days at Solesmes, from Palm Sunday to Easter Tuesday, following all the liturgical services. I was suffering from splitting headaches; each sound hurt me like a blow; by an extreme effort of concentration I was able to rise above this wretched flesh, to leave it to suffer by itself, heaped up in a corner, and to find a pure and perfect joy in the unimaginable beauty of the chanting and the words. . . . It goes without saying that in the course of these services the thought of the Passion of Christ entered into my being once and for all.

[At Solesmes I learned by chance] of the existence of those English poets of the seventeenth century who are named metaphysical. In reading them later on, I discovered the poem called "Love" [by George Herbert]. Often, at the culminating point of a violent headache, I make myself say it over, concentrating all my attention upon it and clinging with all my soul to the tenderness it enshrines. I used to think I was merely reciting it as a beautiful poem, but without my knowing it the recitation had the virtue of a prayer. It was during one of these recitations that . . . Christ himself came down and took possession of me.

Simone Weil, in a letter to Fr. Henri Perrin,
from Marseilles, May 15, 1942

Love

Love bade me welcome; yet my soul drew back,
Guilty of dust and sin.
But quick-eyed Love, observing me grow slack
From my first entrance in,
Drew nearer to me, sweetly questioning
If I lack'd anything.
"A guest," I answer'd, "worthy to be here:"
Love said, "You shall be he."
"I the unkind, ungrateful? Ah, my dear,
I cannot look on Thee."
Love took my hand and smiling did reply,
"Who made the eyes but I?"

"Truth, Lord; but I have marr'd them: let my
     shame
Go where it doth deserve."
"And know you not," says Love, 'Who bore the
     blame?'
"My dear, then I will serve."
"You must sit down," says Love, "and taste my
     meat."
So I did sit and eat.

George Herbert

I
looked for the Dark One
I
found his image
in my heart

I
stood in his court,
my life in his hands,
only his medicine healed.

Mira sold to *Girdhara,*
the world calls her
wayward.

Mirabai

Girdhara means "immovable mountain."

4

JOIN YOUR
HANDS GENTLY

Prayer, say these writers, is not simply a matter of muttering words. It is a state of mind for which you need to prepare yourself. You need to set aside other concerns, quieten what Jean Watt calls the "itch always to be doing," sit still, still your mind, let go. Denise Levertov describes it as a sort of settling and uses the image of grains of sand settling in a well until the water becomes completely clear. Sometimes what follows is distractions, boredom, disquieting thoughts no longer held down by busyness. Sometimes there is a kind of flash—what Ann Lewin compares to the sudden sighting of a kingfisher.

Join your hands gently;
Let the world be placed
Beyond their reach,
Beyond their itch
Always to be doing;
Exempt from speech
This little space thus formed
Between your folded fingers,
Between your going
And your slow return—
This still enclosure
With its own high walls:
Join your hands gently, so,
No lovelier way than this of letting go.

Jean M. Watt

Prayer is like watching for the
Kingfisher. All you can do is
Be where he is likely to appear, and
Wait.
Often, nothing much happens;
There is space, silence and
Expectancy.
No visible sign, only the
Knowledge that he's been there,
And may come again.
Seeing or not seeing cease to matter,
You have been prepared.
But sometimes, when you've almost
Stopped expecting it,
A flash of brightness
Gives encouragement.

Ann Lewin

SANDS OF THE WELL

The golden particles
descend, descend,
traverse the water's
depth and come to rest
on the level bed
of the well until,
the full descent
accomplished, water's
absolute transparence
is complete, unclouded
by constellations
of bright sand.
Is this
the place where you
are brought in meditation?
Transparency
seen for itself —
as if its quality
were not, after all,
to enable
perception *not* of itself?

With a wand
of willow I again
trouble the envisioned pool,
the cloudy nebulae
form and disperse,
the separate
grains again
slowly, slowly
perform their descent,
and again
stillness ensues.

Denise Levertov

Let silence be placed around us,
like a mantle,
Let us enter into it,
as through a small secret door;
stooping,
to emerge into
an acre of peace,
where stillness reigns,
and the voice of God
is ever present.

The voice of God,
in the startled cry
of a refugee child,
waking
in unfamiliar surroundings.
The voice of God,
in the mother,
fleeing with
her treasure
in her arms, who says
"I am here."

The voice of God
in the father
who points to the stars
and says:
"there is our signpost
there is our lantern. Be of good courage."

O Lord, may the mantle of silence
become a cloak of understanding
to warm our hearts in prayer.

Kate McIlhagga

The prayer has great power
Which we pray with all our strength.
It makes an embittered heart mellow,
A sad heart joyful,
A foolish heart wise,
A timid heart bold,
A weak heart strong,
A blind heart clear-seeing,
A cold heart ardent.
It draws God who is great into a heart which is
    small.
It drives the hungry soul up to the fullness of
    God.
It unites the two lovers, God and soul, in a place
    of bliss,
Where they converse long of love.

Mechthild of Magdeburg

IN WHOM WE LIVE AND MOVE
AND HAVE OUR BEING

Birds afloat in air's current,
sacred breath? No, not breath of God,
it seems, but God
the air enveloping the whole
globe of being.
It's we who breathe, in, out, in, the sacred,
leaves astir, our wings
rising, ruffled—but only the saints
take flight. We cower
in cliff-crevice or edge out gingerly
on branches close to the nest. The wind
marks the passage of holy ones riding
that ocean of air. Slowly their wake
reaches us, rocks us.
But storm or still,
numb or poised in attention,
we inhale, exhale, inhale,
encompassed, encompassed.

Denise Levertov

BECOMING DIFFERENT

There can be all the difference in the world between beginning a prayer with 'O Almighty God' and beginning it with 'Thou' breathed to Someone—*there*. We need to practise that, until the Presence becomes so real that He is in deed and truth possessing the very centre where for us the important 'I' stands supreme. . . .

Why is it so difficult to grasp and hold until it possesses you, is right in the centre of you, so that it is integrated in all you do? We must think and wrestle with a thought like this as Jacob did with the Angel. How to receive and pray, grasp and pray, hold on and pray, until I find myself, suddenly, with great surprise, different. Though I am still full of pride and fear and lovelessness—I am different. Not that I have at last conquered my fear only . . . but that at the centre I am different. Like Herschel, the great conductor, who comes into the concert hall and notices all the little irrelevant details that flash before his eyes—a woman's hat, the lights, the small violins—and then the music starts and suddenly he is possessed of something beyond himself, and says: 'I watch my moving hands and they grow strange—what is it moves the body: what am I?'

FINDING WHAT IS

We have to find our way into that rhythm in which God has swung the world—and the moment is always the same. God's calling—my response. His love—my obedience. The greatest good we can set ourselves, with all the passion that is within us, is to see God and give in to what Is.

Florence Allshorn

5

TALKING TO GOD

This is the very heart of what this collection is all about: trying to catch the moment of prayer as prayer—not the experience of thinking about prayer, or trying to ease oneself into doing it, but the timeless instant of self-forgetfulness that oddly leaves us more ourselves than we were before. For most modern people, prayer does not seem an easy or natural activity. Perhaps we are too beset by activity and determined busyness, and perhaps some of us dread prayer, "the silences we strain to fill," or fear that we are simply talking to ourselves. Emily Dickinson complains bitterly that although she is "knocking everywhere," she cannot seem to find the right address. But others have a lovely confidence that they are heard, some of them in the most appalling of circumstances—an unknown writer in Ravensbruck concentration camp, Irina

Ratushinskaya in a KGB prison. Some, like Jane Austen, fasten on safe, sensible words, requests to be helped through the "dailiness" of life; others, like Anne Brontë, suffer the strongest of doubts. "Talking to God" covers a huge range of thoughts and emotions, the whole gamut of human longing and struggle and hope.

PRAYER

At least — to pray — is left — is left —
Oh Jesus — in the Air —
I know not which thy chamber is —
I'm knocking — everywhere —
Thou settest Earthquake in the South —
And Maelstrom in the Sea —
Say, Jesus Christ of Nazareth —
Hast thou no Arm for Me?

Emily Dickinson

God of listening, God of peace,
In our hearts may you increase,
Till our flow of words shall cease,
And we hear you.

Listening is the hardest skill,
Silences we strain to fill,
Far too restless to be still
And just hear you.

If our well-planned words defeat
Words of others that we meet,
Hesitant and incomplete,
Father, hear them.

If the insights that we seek
Come from someone tired and weak,
Looking for a chance to speak,
Help us hear them.

Janet Shepperson

God, the stars are shining:
All eyes have closed in sleep;
The kings have locked their doors.
Each lover is alone, in secret, with the one he
    loves.
And I am here too: alone, hidden from all of
    them —
With You.

Rabi'a the Mystic

We adore the glory and the truth that is God.
Everything within us utters praise.
Our being is formed for this purpose and no other.
All our loves and works find meaning in you.

Jesus, who shows us what God is like,
forgive us our failure to understand
but keep us in your dazzling presence.

For there we learn the nature of holiness
and partake with you in the secret of the godhead.

St. Hilda Community

Dear God,
Are boys really better than girls? I know you
are one, but try to be fair.

From Children's Letters to God

O Lord, remember not only the men and women of goodwill but also those of ill will. But do not remember the suffering they have inflicted upon us; remember the fruits we brought thanks to this suffering, our comradeship, our loyalty, our humility, the courage, the generosity, the greatness of heart which has grown out of this; and when they come to judgment, let all the fruits that we have borne be their forgiveness.

The prayer of an unknown woman,
found on a piece of wrapping paper in
Ravensbruck concentration camp

Take my life, and let it be
consecrated, Lord, to thee;
take my moments and my days,
let them flow in ceaseless praise.

Take my hands, and let them move
at the impulse of thy love;
take my feet, and let them be
swift and beautiful for thee.

Take my voice, and let me sing
always, only, for my King;
take my lips, and let them be
filled with messages for thee.

Take my silver and my gold;
not a mite would I withhold;
take my intellect, and use
ev'ry power as thou shalt choose.

Take my will, and make it thine:
it shall be no longer mine;

take my heart: it is thine own;
it shall be thy royal throne.

Take my love; my Lord, I pour
at thy feet its treasure-store;
take myself, and I will be
ever, only, all for thee.

Frances Ridley Havergal

Lord, hear; Lord, forgive; Lord, do.

Hear what I speak not; forgive what I speak amiss; do what I leave undone; that, not according to my word or my deed, but according to thy mercy and truth, all may issue to thy glory and the good of thy kingdom.

Maria Hare

Think through me, thoughts of God,
My Father, quiet me,
Till in thy holy presence, hushed,
I think my thoughts with thee.

Think through me, thoughts of God,
That always, everywhere,
The stream that through my being flows
May homeward pass in prayer.

Think through me, thoughts of God,
And let my own thoughts be
Lost like the sand-pools on the shore
Of the eternal sea.

Amy Carmichael

While faith is with me, I am blest;
It turns my darkest night to day;
But, while I clasp it to my breast,
I often feel it slide away.

What shall I do if all my love,
My hopes, my toil, are cast away?
And if there be no God above
To hear and bless me when I pray?

Oh, help me, God! For thou alone
Canst my distracted soul relieve.
Forsake it not: it is thine own,
Though weak, yet longing to believe.

Anne Brontë

OFFERING

We hold up our smallness to your greatness,
our fear to your love.
Our tiny act of giving to your great generosity
Ourselves to you.

St. Hilda Community

All as I asked:
There will be for me, will be
(O Lord, thank you!)
A far road
And new people.
There will be for me, will be
A homeless song
And a proud memory.
There will be for me a heaven
Won by honour,
And a cloak beneath my feet.
There will be for me —
Sometimes —
A happy story
Made of wormwood and mint,
A dress, a semi-mask,
A lace dance . . .
And no one will say:
"She saw life and that was it!"

Irina Ratushinskaya, KGB Prison, Kiev,
January 1983

Give us grace, almighty Father, to address thee with all our hearts as well as with our lips. Thou art everywhere present: from thee no secrets can be hidden. Teach us to fix our thoughts on thee, reverently and with love, so that our prayers are not in vain, but are acceptable to thee, now and always. Amen.

Incline us O God to think humbly of ourselves, to be saved only in the examination of our own conduct, to consider our fellow-creatures with kindness, and to judge of all they say and do with the charity which we would desire from them ourselves.

Grant us grace, almighty Father, so to pray as to deserve to be heard.

Jane Austen

At your back,
At your feet,
We shall sit down beside you.
Desiring your waters,
Your seeds,
Your riches,
Your long life,
Your old age,
Desiring these, I set you down quietly.
As you sit here quietly
As I wish, according to my words,
You will take us to be your children.
So that all my children
May be saved.
All will be happy.
Safely they will bring forth their young.
So that all my children may finish their roads
So that they may grow old,
So that you may bless us with life,
So that none of my spring children
May be left standing outside.
So that you may protect us (I have done this).

May our roads be fulfilled;
May we grow old;
May our roads reach to dawn lake;
May we grow old;
May you bless us with life.

Zuni prayer

Father, we thank thee for our happiness, for our great gift of life: for the wonder and bloom of the world. We bless thee that it takes a very little thing to make us happy, yet so great a thing to satisfy us that only thyself canst do it, for thou alone art greater than our hearts. We bless thee for thy calling which is so high that no man can perfectly attain unto it, and for thy grace which stoops so low that none of us can ever fall too low for it. Above all we bless thee that thou didst send thy Son, Jesus Christ our Lord, for having seen him we have seen thee, whose truth doth ever warm and whose grace doth ever keep.

Helen Waddell

All this day, O Lord,
let me touch as many lives as possible for thee;
and every life I touch, do thou by thy Spirit
    quicken,
whether through the word I speak,
the prayer I breathe, or the life I live.

Mary Sumner

Spirit of God, that moved of old
Upon the waters' darkened face,
Come, when our faithless hearts are cold,
And stir them with an inward grace.

Thou that art power and peace combined,
All highest strength, all purest love,
The rushing of the mighty wind,
The brooding of the gentle dove.

Come give us still thy powerful aid,
And urge us on, and keep us thine;
Nor leave the hearts that once were made
Fit temples for thy grace divine;

Nor let us quench thy sevenfold light;
But still with softest breathings stir
Our wayward souls, and lead us right,
O Holy Ghost, the comforter.

Cecil Frances Alexander

Let us make our way together, Lord, wherever you go I must go, and through whatever you pass, there too will I pass.

St. Teresa of Ávila

How lovely are thy holy groves
God of heaven and earth
My soul longs and faints
for the circle of thy trees.
My heart and my flesh
sing with joy to thee
O God of life.

May all things move and be moved in me
all know and be known in me
May all creation
dance for joy within me.

Chinook prayer

Lord, thou knowest what I want,
if it be thy will that I have it,
and if it be not thy will,
good Lord, do not be displeased,
for I want nothing which you do not want.

Julian of Norwich

6

RITUALS, CEREMONIES, AND SEASONS

If prayer can be difficult as a lonely exercise, it can be very different when shared with a community of other believers. The experience of worshiping in a synagogue, church, or temple can sweep the individual along in ritual, music, and prayer. Sitting in zazen in a Zen monastery can bring the sitter to a depth of meditation hard to achieve alone. Rituals performed at home, such as the lighting of the Sabbath candles, also have profound meaning. Doing something, as opposed to saying something, feels helpful, as Roman Catholics with their rosaries and Tibetans with their prayer wheels also discover. Most religions, if not all, also have a sense of the times of day and the seasons of the year, of particular prayers said and rituals associated with the rising or setting of the sun, with changes in the climate, and with growth or decline in the natural world. Festivals, too, are intimately caught up in our sense of climate, as Christmas, at the heart of winter in the cold Northern hemisphere with its emphasis on light and fire, reminds many Westerners. Festivals are sometimes mixed with bits of paganism, which hint at the older festivals that preceded them, fertility rites, and earth religions. Perhaps this makes them more rather than less effective, as they touch ancestral responses in the worshipers. Cooking, too, is as important a ritual as any in many religious festivals, with classic dishes associated with particular meanings. I have included a Jewish recipe to remind us of this. Food, so often prepared by women, itself demonstrates transformation as raw materials are changed into something very different. In Judaism, meals are intimately part of religious practice; they are symbolic, in the case of charoseth and other foods, of the stories that give meaning.

Alongside traditional religious practices, however, there has been in some women's groups a conscious return to the cult of primitive goddesses—of the "Great Goddess," as some prefer to say—along with rituals of invocation. "The Charge of the Goddess" in this section is a moving hymn to neopaganism.

Sabbath Candlelighting

May our hearts be lifted,
our spirits refreshed,
as we light the Sabbath candles.

Sanctification over the Wine for Sabbath Eve

There was evening and there was morning, the sixth day.
The heavens and earth were complete, with all their host.
Genesis 1:31–2:1

Let us bless the source of life
that ripens fruit on the vine
as we hallow the seventh day—
the Sabbath day—
in remembrance of creation,
for the Sabbath is first
among holy days,
recalling the exodus
and the covenant.

Handwashing before the Meal

Washing the hands, we call to mind
the holiness of body.

Blessing before the Meal

Let us bless the source of life
that brings forth bread from the earth.

Blessing after the Meal
Let us acknowledge the source of life,
source of all nourishment.

May we protect the bountiful earth
that it may continue to sustain us,

and let us seek sustenance
for all who dwell in the world.

Marcia Falk

CHANUKAH

We come to drive away darkness,
in our hands are light and fire.
Each one is a small light,
and all of us are a mighty light.
Away with darkness, away with blackness!
Away before the light.

Sarah Levy

CHRISTMAS

We stand at the turning of the year, the time of death and birth, of darkness and light, of sadness and joy, and we remember the baby born in a stable who pours glory upon our lives. As we give presents to one another we recognise the love present in our world, a love that redeems the cruelty, pain and fear.

Monica Furlong

AN ASH WEDNESDAY PRAYER

O God,
you have made us for yourself,
and against your longing there is no defence.
Mark us with your love,
and release in us a passion for your justice
in our disfigured world;
that we may turn from our guilt and face you,
our heart's desire. Amen.

Janet Morley

LENT

Dragons lurk in desert spaces
penetrating the mind with evil claw.
Serpents' teeth seek out the chinks
insidiously, relentlessly gnawing on the bone;
searching out the interstices of muscle and sinew.

Such is the pain of the wilderness.
Alone, alone, alone,
Christ sits
in the waste place of abandoned pleas and
     questions
until exhausted
finally
at last
the realisation
comes
that in the end
there is only
God.

In the nighttime of our fears,
and in our time of questioning,
Be present, ever present God.
Be present with those
camped out in the fields of hopelessness,
with refugees and homeless,
those who live lives of quiet desperation.
Be present until the desert places
blossom like the rose
and hope is born again.

Kate McIlhagga

THE CHARGE OF THE GODDESS

I who am the beauty of the green earth and the white moon among the stars and the mysteries of the waters, I call upon your soul to arise and come unto me. For I am the soul of nature that gives life to the universe. From Me all things proceed and unto Me they must return. Let My worship be in the heart that rejoices, for behold—all acts of love and pleasure are My rituals. Let there be beauty and strength, power and compassion, honor and humility, mirth and reverence within you. And you who seek to know Me, know that your seeking and yearning will avail you not, unless you know the Mystery: for if that which you seek, you find not within yourself, you will never find it without. For behold, I have been with you from the beginning, and I am that which is attained at the end of desire.

Doreen Valiente, adapted by Starhawk

THE BAPTISM BLESSING

Thou Being who inhabitest the heights
Imprint thy blessing betimes,
Remember Thou the child of my body,
In Name of the Father of peace;
When the priest of the King
On him put the water of meaning,
Grant him the blessing of the Three
Who fill the heights.
The blessing of the Three
Who fill the heights.

Sprinkle down upon him Thy grace,
Give Thou to him virtue and growth,
Give Thou to him flocks and possessions,
Sense and reason void of guile,
Angel wisdom in his day,
That he may stand without reproach
In Thy presence.
He may stand without reproach
In Thy presence.

Gaelic, Anonymous

HARVEST

We dare not ask you bless our harvest feast
Till it is spread for poorest and for least.
We dare not bring our harvest gifts to you
Unless our hungry brothers share them too.

Not only at this time, Lord, every day
Those whom you love are dying while we pray.
Teach us to do with less, and so to share
From our abundance more than we can spare.

Now with this harvest plenty round us piled,
Show us the Christ in every starving child;
Speak, as you spoke of old in Galilee,
'You feed, or you refuse, not them but me!'

Lilian Cox

CHAROSETH

Apples, ½ pound
Raisins, 2 ounces
Almonds, 2 ounces
Cinnamon

Peel and core the apples and chop finely, together with the almonds and raisins. Mix together, adding cinnamon to taste. Then form into a neat block and place in a glass dish, or roll into tiny balls and coat with chopped nuts.

Florence Greenberg

At the Passover meal, Charoseth represents the mortar with which the children of Israel built the slave cities for Pharaoh. The bitter memory has been transformed into a sweet.

7

LIVING IS DAILINESS

Dailiness, say many of the holy men and women of the world, is the vehicle through which God expresses himself in our world. The routines of work, travel, family, and friendship are the places where, if anywhere, we shall find God. Judith Wright speaks of the astonishing moment, known perhaps to everyone, where, unlooked for, an extraordinary awareness suddenly "slants a sudden laser through the common day." It is the small as well as the great actions of our everyday life that make us, for good or ill, the people that we are. Today, as St. Thérèse of Lisieux observes, is in a sense the only day we have, or may have, to love God and our neighbor. Work, which so often for women has meant domestic work, is an instrument of giving and a tool of hospitality. The stranger whom we house or feed may turn out to be the Divine. For the

Gaelic peoples of the Scottish isles, everyday work —kindling the fire, milking the cow, working the loom —was full of religious meaning. Angels and archangels watched over it all. Although many of the prayers here come from the Christian tradition, they speak to us all as examples of the strong sense of the importance of the everyday that is shared by so many religious traditions.

Living is dailiness, a simple bread
that's worth the eating. But I have known a wine,
a drunkenness that can't be spoken or sung
without betraying it. Far past Yours or Mine,
even past Ours, it has nothing at all to say;
it slants a sudden laser through the common day.
It seems to have nothing to do with things at all,
requires another element or dimension.
Not contemplation brings it; it merely happens,
past expectation and beyond intention;
takes over the depth of flesh, the inward eye,
is there, then vanishes. Does not live or die,
because it occurs beyond the here and now,
positives, negatives, what we hope and are.
Not even being in love, or making love,
brings it. It lunges a sword from a dark star.
Maybe there was once a word for it. Call it grace.
I have seen it, once or twice, through a human
        face.

Judith Wright

Now, into the keeping of God I put
All doings of today.
All disappointments,
hindrances,
forgotten things,
negligences.
All gladness and beauty,
love,
delight,
achievement.
All that people have done for me,
All that I have done for them,
my work and my prayers.

And I commit all the people whom I love
to his shepherding,
to his healing and restoring,
to his calling and making;
Through Jesus Christ our Lord.

Margaret Cropper

My life is an instant,
An hour which passes by;
My life is a moment
Which I have no power to stay.
You know, O my God,
That to love you here on earth—
I have only today.

St. Thérèse of Lisieux

God give me work
Till my life shall end
And life
Till my work is done.

On the grave of the writer Winifred Holtby

BLESSING OF THE KINDLING

I will kindle my fire this morning
In presence of the holy angels of heaven,
In presence of Ariel of the loveliest form,
In presence of Uriel of the myriad charms,
Without malice, without jealousy, without envy,
Without fear, without terror of any one under
    the sun,
But the Holy Son of God to shield me.

God, kindle Thou in my heart within
A flame of love to my neighbour,
To my foe, to my friend, to my kindred all,
To the brave, to the knave, to the thrall,
On Son of the loveliest Mary,
From the lowliest thing that liveth,
To the Name that is highest of all.

Gaelic, Anonymous

Every day is a fresh beginning,
Listen my soul to the glad refrain.
    And, spite of old sorrows
    And older sinning,
    Troubles forecasted
    And possible pain,
Take heart with the day and begin again.

Susan Coolidge

FOLDING THE SHEETS

You and I will fold the sheets
Advancing towards each other
From Burma, from Lapland.

From India where the sheets have been washed
    in the river
And pounded upon stones:
Together we will match the corners.

From China where women on either side of the
    river
Have washed their pale cloth in the White Stone
    Shallows
'Under the shining moon.'

We meet as though in the formal steps of a dance
To fold the sheets together, put them to air
In wind, in sun over bushes, or by the fire.

We stretch and pull from one side and then the

other—
Your turn. Now mine.
We fold them and put them away until they are
    needed.

A wish for all people when they lie down in
    bed—
Smooth linen, cool cotton, the fragrance and stir
    of herbs
And the faint but perceptible scent of sweet clear
    water.

Rosemary Dobson

I should like a great lake of finest ale
For the King of Kings
I should like a table of the choicest food
For the family of heaven
Let the ale be made from the fruits of faith
And the food be forgiving love.

I should welcome the poor to my feast
For they are God's children
I should welcome the sick to my feast
For they are God's joy.
Let the poor sit with Jesus at the highest place
And the sick dance with the angels.

God bless the poor
God bless the sick
And bless the human race.
God bless our food.
God bless our drink.
All homes, O God, embrace.

St. Bridget of Kildare

8

MOTHERS AND FOREBEARS

Make us worthy, Lord, to serve our fellow-men throughout the world who live and die in poverty and hunger.

Give them, through our hands, this day their daily bread, and by our understanding love, give peace and joy.

Prayer of Mother Teresa

A RUNE OF HOSPITALITY

I saw a stranger today.
I put food for him in the eating-place
And drink in the drinking-place
And music in the listening-place.
In the Holy Name of the Trinity
He blessed myself and my house
My goods and my family.
And the lark said in her warble
Often, often, often
Goes Christ in the stranger's guise.
O, oft and oft and oft,
Goes Christ in the stranger's guise.

Christ has no body now on earth but yours;
yours are the only hands with which he can do
    his work,
yours are the only feet with which he can go
    about the world,
yours are the only eyes through which his
    compassion
can shine forth upon a troubled world.
Christ has no body now on earth but yours.

St. Teresa of Ávila

The number of named women in history until modern times is very few. The ones who are named tend to be divine, or semidevine. As such, they are a source of inspiration like many of the women named in this section, or they were associated with, or relatives of, famous men, like Miriam, the sister of Moses. A very few, like Sappho, or Naomi and Ruth, or Hatshepsut, have found their own way into history, achieving in some cases a kind of iconic status. Since they are relatively few they are treasured as part of women's history, often connected with religion, and, like the other named women, they lift a curtain, however briefly, on the lost world of women's experience.

THE SONG OF MIRIAM

For when the horses of Pharaoh with his chariots and his horsemen went into the sea, the Lord brought back the waters of the sea upon them; but the people of Israel walked on dry ground in the midst of the sea. Then Miriam, the prophetess, the sister of Aaron, took a timbrel in her hand; and all the women went out after her with timbrels and dancing. And Miriam sang to them:

"Sing to the Lord, for he has triumphed
    gloriously;
the horse and rider he has thrown into the sea."

Exodus 15:19–21

RUTH AND NAOMI

And Ruth said, Intreat me not to leave thee, or to return from following after thee: for whither thou goest, I will go; and where thou lodgest, I will lodge: thy people shall be my people, and thy God my God:

Where thou diest, will I die, and there will I be buried: the Lord do so to me, and more also, if aught but death part thee and me.

Ruth 1:16–17

QUEEN HATSHEPSUT

By my life, by the love of Ra and the favour of my father Amen. . . . I bear the white crown, I am diademed with the red crown. . . . I rule over this land like the son of Isis, I am mighty like the son of Nu. . . . I shall be for ever like the star which changeth not. He gave me my royal power over Egypt and the red country, all the foreign lands are under my feet . . . all the marvels and all the precious things of this land, they are presented to my palace altogether . . . turquoise of the land of Reshut—they bring to me the choicest things from the oasis of Testesu, acacia, juniper, merwood . . . all the good woods of the divine land. . . . Tribute is brought to me from the land of the Tahennu in ivory, seven hundred tusks. . . . She lives, she is stable, she is in good health, she is joyous as well as her double on the throne of Horus of the living like the sun, for ever and ever.

Hatshepsut

HYMN TO APHRODITE

I sing of Aphrodite, the lover's goddess,
beautiful, gold-crowned, a blossom
riding the seafoam, resting on the wind.
She comes ashore, and women
in gold bracelets meet her, bearing
silken garments for her lovely body,
copper rings for her shell ears,
chains of gold for her silver breasts.

They lead her from the seashore.
Do not look upon her! Your eyes
would dazzle from such beauty.
But you do not need to see her.
You already know her. It is she
who moves you in your dance.
She is the music of your life.
Do you need to ask her name?
Call her Love. Call her Joy.
Call her golden Aphrodite.

She is the moment when body
knits to body and the world flowers.
She enlivens everything: plants
in the meadow, the ocean's fish,

animals hidden in the forest,
birds tumbling on the wind.
She is our darling, who under
the wheeling stars makes all
things blossom and bear fruit.
At her approach storms clear,
dark clouds dissolve to blue,
sweet earth and all the oceans
smile, and her light dances brilliant
through the flourishing world.

Homer, adapted by Patricia Monaghan

WISDOM

Doth not wisdom cry? and understanding put
forth her voice?

She standeth in the top of high places, by the
way in the places of the paths.

She crieth at the gates, at the entry of the city, at
the coming in at the doors.

Unto you, O men, I call; and my voice is to the
sons of men.

O ye simple, understand wisdom: and ye fools, be
of an understanding heart.

Hear; for I will speak of excellent things; and the
opening of my lips shall be right things. . . .

Receive my instruction, and not silver; and
knowledge rather than choice gold.

For wisdom is better than rubies; and all the
things that may be desired are not to be
compared to it.

I wisdom dwell with prudence, and find out
knowledge of witty inventions. . . .

Counsel is mine, and sound wisdom: I am
understanding; I have strength.

By me kings reign, and princes decree justice.

By me princes rule, and nobles, even all the
judges of the earth.

I love them that love me, and those that seek me
early shall find me.

Riches and honour are with me; yea, durable
riches and righteousness.

My fruit is better than gold, yea, than fine gold;
and my revenue than choice silver. . . .

The Lord possessed me in the beginning of his
way, before his works of old.

I was set up from everlasting, from the
beginning, or ever the earth was.

When there were no depths, I was brought forth;
when there were no fountains abounding with
water.

Before the mountains were settled, before the
hills was I brought forth:

While as yet he had not made the earth, nor the
fields, nor the highest part of the dust of the
world.

When he prepared the heavens, I was there:
when he set a compass upon the face of the
depth:

When he established the clouds above: when he
strengthened the fountains of the deep:

When he gave to the sea his decree, that the
    waters should not pass his commandment:
when he appointed the foundations of the earth:
Then I was by him, as one brought up with him:
    and I was daily his delight, rejoicing always
    before him;
Rejoicing in the habitable part of his earth; and
    my delights were with the sons of men. . . .
Blessed is the man that heareth me, watching
    daily at my gates, waiting at the posts of my
    doors.
For whoso findeth me findeth life, and shall
    obtain favour of the Lord.
But he that sinneth against me, wrongeth his own
    soul.

Proverbs 8

GREETING SHEKINAH

Two figures face each other,
Sitting close to the earth in the old way;
Outside in the early morn
The women face each other,
Eye to eye, smile to smile,
Squatting over the earth,
Backs curved like earthen pots.
So gracefully they sit,
Pouring water over each other's hands.
Fire pales as the sun rises;
The spice of dew consecrates the hour.
"Shekinah of the sun, Shekinah of the moon,
We greet You with our morning song,
We greet You with the washing of hands,
We greet you with our dawn fire.
Shekinah of the morning star, Shekinah of
    the dew,
We welcome You as the running deer,
Our feet swift in dancing.
We welcome You as the golden eagle,

Our hands spread in prayer.
We welcome You as the shimmering stream,
Our spirit flowing to the sea of Your delight.
We bless the day with our rising smoke.
Let our prayers ascend to the skies.
Let our prayers touch the earth.
Shalom Achoti, shalom Sister,
All life sings Your song."

Lynn Gottlieb

THE HYMN TO HESTIA

Hestia,
you who received the highest honor,
to have your seat forever
in the enormous houses of all the gods
and all the men who walk on the earth,
it is a beautiful gift you have received,
it is a beautiful honor.
Without you, mankind would have no feasts,
since no one could begin the first and last drink
of honey-like wine without an offering
to Hestia.

Homer, translated by Charles Boer

KALI

Kali
queen of fatality, she
determines the destiny
of things, nemesis.
the permanent guest
within ourselves.
woman of warfare,
of the chase, bitch
of blood sacrifice and death.
dread mother, the mystery
ever present in us and
outside us, the
terrible hindu woman God
Kali
who is black.

Lucille Clifton

IN THE YOUNG SPRING EVENING

In the young spring evening
The moon is shining full
Girls form a circle
As though round an altar

And their feet perform
Rhythmical steps
Like the soft feet of Cretan girls
Must once have danced.

Round and round an altar of love
Designing a circle
In the delicate flowering grass

The stars that are shining
Around the beautiful moon
Hide their own bright faces
When She, at Her fullest
Paints the earth with Her
Silvery light.

Now, while we are dancing
Come! Join us!

Sweet joy, revelry,
Bright light!

Inspire us, muses
Oh, you with the beautiful hair.

Sappho, translated by Charoula

THE MARTYRDOM OF PERPETUA AND FELICITY IN THE ROMAN CIRCUS

Now dawned the day of their victory, and they [the group of Christians] went forth from the prison into the amphitheatre as it were into heaven, cheerful and bright of countenance; if they trembled at all, it was for joy, not for fear. Perpetua followed behind, glorious of presence, as a true spouse of Christ and darling of God; at whose piercing look all cast down their eyes. Felicity likewise, rejoicing that she had [now] borne her child in safety, that she might fight with the beasts, came now from blood to blood, from the midwife to the gladiator, to wash after her travail in a second baptism. And when they had been brought to the gate and were being compelled to put on, the men the dress of the priests of Saturn, the women the dress of the priestesses of Ceres, the noble Perpetua remained of like firmness to the end, and would not. For she said: For this cause came we willingly unto this, that our liberty might not be obscured. For this cause we have devoted our lives, that we might do not such thing as this; this we agreed with you. Injustice acknowledged justice; the tribune suffered that they should be brought forth as they were, without more ado. Perpetua began to sing. . . . When they came into Hilarion's sight, they began to say to Hilarion . . . 'Thou judgest us, and God thee.'

For the women the devil had made ready a most savage cow, prepared for this purpose against all custom; for even in this beast he would mock their sex. They were stripped therefore and made to put on nets; and so they were brought forth. The people shuddered, seeing one a tender girl, the other her breasts yet dropping from her late childbearing. So they were called back and dressed in loose robes. Perpetua was first thrown, and fell upon her loins. And when she had sat upright, her robe being rent at the side, she drew it over to cover her thigh, mindful rather of modesty than of pain. Next, looking for a pin, she likewise pinned up her dishevelled hair; for it was not meet that a martyr should suffer with hair dishevelled, lest she should seem to grieve in her glory. So she stood up, and when she saw Felicity smitten down, she went up and gave her her hand and raised her up. And both of them stood up together. . . . Perpetua called to her brother, and another catechumen and spoke to them saying 'Stand fast in the faith, and love ye all one another, and be not offended because of our passion.' [The people called that the Christians, a number of them mauled by beasts, should be despatched by a swordsman]. . . . Perpetua was pierced between the bones and shrieked out; and when the swordman's hand wandered still (for he was a novice), herself set it upon her own neck. Perchance so great a woman could not else have been slain . . . had she not herself so willed it.

The Passion of Perpetua and Felicity, c. 202 A.D.,
Acta Sanctorum 1688

Hilarion was the Procurator who had condemned Perpetua and the other Christians.

THE TWO SISTERS—THE DREAMING

On the Island of the Spirits of the Dead,
one of two sisters talks.
"We must make a canoe and follow the way
the sun walks."
They've filled the canoe with sacred 'rannga'
    things,
and paddled away into the night
singing ritual songs.

"Sister, look back!" the first sister calls.
"Do you see the morning star?"
Her sister looks out along their wake.
"Nothing. Nothing's there."

The little sister has fallen asleep.
Again her sister calls,
"Sister, look back for the morning star."
"Nothing. Nothing at all."

A spear of light is thrown across
the sea and lies far

ahead of the sisters' course.
"Sister, the morning star."

The sun comes up and walks the sky.
A fish with whiskers swims
ahead, and leaps out of the sea,
while the sisters sing.

Day and night, and day and night,
the sisters are gone
with the morning star and the leaping fish
and the sky-walking sun.

The sisters, hoar with dried salt spray,
the semen of the sea,
make landfall where the parrots scream
From paperbark trees.
The sisters beach the bark canoe,
unload the 'rannga' things.
They thrust one in the earth. From there
the first goanna comes.
They've gone inland. Their digging sticks
make sacred springs.

They leave behind them 'rannga' forms
for all living things.
Out gathering food, the sisters have hung
their dilly-bags in a tree.
While they're away, men come and steal
their sacred ceremonies.
The sisters hear men singing and
song-sticks' "tjong-tjong."
"Cover your ears. We cannot hear
the sacred song.

O, all our sacred ceremonies
belong now to the men.
We must gather food, and bear
and rear children."

Manoowa

9

THE PLACE OF
SELF-DISCOVERY

These moving poems and prayers describe the lives of women who have struggled and have felt pain and despair—in one case to the point of suicide, in another possibly to the point of madness—and have found a way through. Oodgeroo of Noonuccal (the fine Australian poet more usually known as Kath Walker) notes the way that love and pain are inextricable: "light and sister shade." For the Buddhist women Mutta, Nanduttara, and Siha, there has been the cutting away of lives that degraded and destroyed them, and the extraordinary discovery that they are free. The themes are familiar ones: the constriction of guilt in women's lives, the desperate attempt to cling to love, and the consequent release at the moment of letting go. It is an unfamiliar but very convincing study of salvation, which perhaps is something like what Dawna Markova suggests is "the lived life."

The desert waits,
ready for those who come,
who come obedient to the Spirit's leading;
or who are driven,
because they will not come any other way.

The desert always waits,
ready to let us know who we are —
the place of self-discovery.
And whilst we fear, and rightly,
the loneliness and emptiness and harshness,
we forget the angels,
whom we cannot see for our blindness,
but who come when God decides
that we need their help;
when we are ready
for what they can give us.

Ruth Burgess

I will not die an unlived life,
I will not go in fear
Of falling or catching fire,
I choose to inhabit my days,
To allow my living to open to me,
To make me less afraid,
More accessible,
To loosen my heart
Until it becomes a wing,
A torch, a promise.
I chose to risk my significance:
To live.
So that which comes to me as seed,
Goes to the next as blossom,
And that which comes to me as blossom,
Goes on as fruit.

Dawna Markova

MUTTA SPEAKS

I'm free. Ecstatically free
I'm free from three crooked things:
the mortar,
the pestle
and my hunchbacked husband
All that drags me back is cut-cut!

Mutta, a Therigata nun

SONG

Life is ours in vain
Lacking love, which never
Counts the loss or gain.
But remember, ever
Love is linked with pain.

Light and sister shade
Shape each mortal morrow
Seek not to evade
Love's companion, Sorrow,
And be not dismayed.

Grief is not in vain,
It's for our completeness.
If the fates ordain
Love to bring life sweetness'
Welcome too its pain.

Oodgeroo of the tribe Noonuccal (Kath Walker)

I used to worship
fire, the moon, sun,
all the gods
I used to go down
to the riverbanks
for the bathing rites
I took holy vows
shaved half my head
slept on the ground
wouldn't eat food after sundown
Then I decked myself
out with many ornaments
baths, unguents, massage —
you name it —
Tried everything
to stave off death
I was a slave to my body
Then I really "got" it
saw my body as it really is
went homeless
Lust? Sex?

Forget it
All that binds me head and foot
is loosened.

Nanduttara, a Therigata nun

THE FORMER COURTESAN VIMALA

I used to be puffed up
high on good looks
intoxicated by a rosy complexion
voluptuous figure
I was haughty, vain,
looked down on other women
I was young
All painted up
I stood at the brothel door
like a hunter laying snares,
showing my wares —
Here are my breasts, a thigh
(lifts a skirt)
I conjured, mocked, seduced —
Today I'm bald
Clad in the outer robe, I go begging
Sitting at the foot of a tree,

I no longer discriminate
All ties have been cut
I said, cut.

Vimala

Vimala was converted by one of the Buddha's disciples, whom
she had tried in vain to seduce. She became a lay believer.

SIHA
WHO THOUGHT OF SUICIDE,
BUT GAVE IT UP

Distracted
too passionate
dumb about
the way things work
I was stung and tossed
by memories
Haunted, you could say
I went on like this,
wandering for seven years
Thin, pale, desperate
Nothing to hold me
Taking a rope
I went to the woods
Hanging is better
than this low life.
The noose was strong
I tied it to the branch of a tree
flung it round my neck
when suddenly—look—
it snapped!
Not my neck
my *heart* was free.

Siha, a Therigata nun

THE EDGE

Three times to the world's end I went,
Three times returned as one who brings
Tidings of light beyond the dark
But voiceless stays, still marvelling.

After great pain I had great joy
Three times that never else I knew;
The last reflection of its light
Fades from the pupils of my eyes.

Webbed by the world again I walk
The mazy paths that women tread
Watchful lest any harm should come
To those who journeyed back with me.

But still, as Lazarus who was born
Again beyond the edge of death,
I see the world half otherwise
And tremble at its mysteries.

Rosemary Dobson

10

THE SONG IS GONE

This section is full of the sense of grieving and loss—grieving for the lost way of life of Aboriginal peoples and for the tragedy of lost animal and plant species, which in turn has affected vulnerable peoples. "If the earth is spoiled," says the Yoruba poem, "it cannot be repaired." There is also anger about the way greed for profit has destroyed much that was precious.

BORA RING

The song is gone; the dance
is secret with the dancers in the earth,
the ritual useless, and the tribal story
lost in an alien tale.

Only the grass stands up
to mark the dancing-ring: the apple gums
posture and mime a past corroboree,
murmur a broken chant.

The hunter is gone: the spear
is splintered underground; the painted bodies
a dream the world breathed sleeping and forgot.
The nomad feet are still.

Only the rider's heart
halts at a sightless shadow, an unsaid word

that fastens in the blood the ancient curse,
the fear as old as Cain.

Judith Wright

The bora ring is the ceremonial space in which ritual
Aboriginal dances were performed.

WE ARE GOING

For Grannie Coolwell

They came in to the little town
A semi-naked band subdued and silent,
All that remained of their tribe.
They came to the place of their old bora ground
Where now the many white men hurry about
    like ants.
Notice of estate agent reads: 'Rubbish May Be
    Tipped Here'.
Now it half covers the traces of the old bora ring.
They sit and are confused, they cannot say their
    thoughts:
'We are as strangers here now, but the white
    tribe are the strangers.
We belong here, we are of the old ways.
We are the corroboree and the bora ground,
We are the old sacred ceremonies, the laws of the
    elders.

We are the wonder tales of Dream Time, the
    tribal legends told.
We are the past, the hunts and the laughing
    games, the wandering camp fires.
We are the lightning bolt over Gaphembah Hill
Quick and terrible,
And the Thunder after him, that loud fellow.
We are the quiet daybreak paling the dark
    lagoon.
We are the shadow-ghosts creeping back as the
    camp fires burn low.
We are nature and the past, all the old ways
Gone now and scattered.
The scrubs are gone, the hunting and the
    laughter.
The eagle is gone, the emu and the kangaroo are
    gone from this place.
The bora ring is gone.
The corroboree is gone.
And we are going.

Oodgeroo of the tribe Noonuccal (Kath Walker)

Show us, O God, how to love not only animals, birds and all green and growing things, but the soil, air and water by which we live, so that we may not exploit or pollute them for our own profit or convenience.

Help us to cherish these necessities for our survival; and guide those in authority to ensure that the human spirit may not be starved in pursuit of material comfort and wealth.

Phoebe Hesketh

Lord, purge our eyes to see
Within the seed a tree,
within the glowing egg a bird,
Within the shroud a butterfly.
Till, taught by such we see
Beyond all creatures, thee
And hearken to thy tender word
And hear its "Fear not; it is I."

Christina Rossetti

AFTER EDEN

We ate not flesh in Eden, but afterwards,
when things got hard, we forgot
the peaceful kinship of that ancient kingdom.
As our teeth sank into their flesh
we had to deny them. So we said
they had no souls, no reason, no thumbs,
no speech. We were so different. We made
a chain of things to protect us — fire, medicine,
our locking houses, many kinds of clothes.
And we renamed them — farm product, fur crop,
renewable resource. Pray that we will see
their faces again in the mirror of creation,
the miracle of animals, their clear eyes
meaning more than profit to our own!

Jean Pearson

Enjoy the earth gently
For if the earth is spoiled
It cannot be repaired
Enjoy the earth gently.

Yoruba prayer

Helper of all who are helpless,
we call on you in times of stress
and in times of devastation.
Pick up the broken pieces
of our hearts, our homes, our history
and restore them to the way they were,
or give us the means of starting over
when everything seems lost.
O God, our help in ages past,
we place all our hope in you.

Miriam Therese Winter

11

BIRTH AND DEATH

At Maes Howe, on mainland Orkney in the Northern Isles of Scotland, there is an ancient tomb, probably built to take the bodies of chieftains and nobles. It is entered through a long narrow tunnel, which one has to bend double to walk through. Only when you reach the inner space, and can stand up, do you realize that the whole is constructed rather like a womb. The dead chieftain who once, like all the rest of us, left the peace of the womb and made his passage out into the daylight has now made his journey in reverse. Before visiting Maes Howe I had never thought to link birth and death in that way, but I found it a welcome idea. Death is a kind of second birth, only we do not know where it will take us, any more than the baby in the womb knows where it is going. So I decided to combine birth and death in this section.

For most women until recent times, giving birth was a journey through the valley of the shadow of death, in which they knew they might easily lose their lives. The passionate Gaelic prayer to the much-loved saint Bride must have been a comfort. There is another heartfelt invocation to a baby who, with the infinite pathos of the very young, was not going to live to discover the world. The two bitter Aboriginal mourning songs, while painful to read, catch the anger and helplessness of bereavement with a force and clarity that many of us will recognize.

A BIRTHING PRAYER TO ST. BRIDE

There came to me assistance,
Mary fair and Bride;
As Anna bore Mary,
As Mary bore Christ,
As Eile bore John the Baptist
Without flaw in him,
Aid thou me in mind unbearing,
   Aid me, O Bride!

As Christ was conceived of Mary
Full perfect on every hand,
Assist thou me, foster-mother,
The conception to bring from the bone;
As thou didst aid the Virgin of joy,
Without gold, without corn, without kine,
Aid thou me, great is my sickness,
   Aid me, O Bride.

Gaelic, Anonymous

TO BE SUNG BY THE ONE
WHO FIRST TAKES THE CHILD
FROM ITS MOTHER

Newborn, on the naked sand
Nakedly lay it.
Next to the earth mother,
That it may know her,
Having good thoughts of her, the food giver.

Newborn, we tenderly
In our arms take it,
Making good thoughts.
House-god, be entreated,
That it may grow from childhood to manhood,
Happy, contented,
Beautifully walking
The trail to old age.
Having good thoughts of the earth its mother,
That she may give it the fruits of her being.
Newborn, on the naked sand
Nakedly lay it.

Pueblo song

THE NEWBORN

My little son, I have cast you out
To hang heels upward, wailing over a world
With walls too wide.
My faith till now, and now my love:
No walls too wide for that to fill, no depth
Too great for all you hide.

I love, not knowing what I love,
I give, though ignorant for whom
The history and power of a name.
I conjure with it, like a novice
Summoning unknown spirits: answering me
You take the word and tame it.

Even as the gift of life
You take the famous name you did not choose
And make it new.
You and the name exchange a power:
Its history is changed, becoming yours,
And yours by this: who calls this, calls you.

Strong vessel of peace, and plenty promised,
Into whose unsounding depths I pour
This alien power;
Frail vessel launched with a shawl for sail,
Whose guiding spirit keeps his needle-quivering
Poise between trust and terror,
And stares amazed to find himself alive;
This is the means by which you say *I am,*
Not to be lost till all is lost,
When at the sight of God you say *I am nothing,*
And find, forgetting name and speech at last,
A home not mine, dear outcast.

Anne Ridler

ELEGY

I am going home with thee
To thy home! to thy home!
I am going home with thee
To thy home of winter.

I am going home with thee
To thy home! to thy home!
I am going home with thee
To thy home of autumn,
of spring and of summer.

I am going home with thee,
Thou child of my love,
To thine eternal bed
To thy perpetual sleep.

I am going home with thee,
Thou child of my love,
To the dear Son of blessings,
To the Father of grace.

Anonymous

There, in that other world, what waits for me?
What shall I find after that other birth?
No stormy, tossing, foaming, smiling sea,
But a new earth.

No sun to mark the changing of the days,
No slow, soft falling of the alternate night,
No moon, no star, no light upon my ways,
Only the Light.

No gray cathedral, wide and wondrous fair,
That I may tread where all my fathers trod.
Nay, nay, my soul, no house of God is there,
But only God.

Mary Coleridge

TWO ABORIGINAL WOMEN'S MOURNING SONGS

The blowflies buzz . . .

Ah, the blowfly is whining there, its maggots are
    eating the flesh.
The blowflies buzz, their feet stray over the
    corpse . . .
The buzzing goes on and on . . .
Who is it, eating there, whose flesh are they
    eating? . . .
Ah my daughter, come back here to me!
Ah, our daughter was taken ill—
You didn't sing for her, as a father should!
You are foolish and silly, you sing only to please
    the ears of women!
You like to lie close to a young girl, a virgin, and
    give her a child!
You will not stay in one place;
Here and there, all over the place, you go among
    the camps,

You go walking hither and thither, looking for
    sweethearts.
Ah, before it was here that you used to stay.
You should be ashamed to do that before all these
    strangers!
Presently I will take up a knife and cut you!
(B says: 'This is all that I do: I get food to eat,
    and tobacco to smoke!')
No, you go to sit down beside some woman,
You sit close, close beside her . . .
Ah, my lost, sick child—ah, the blowflies!
Soon I will hit that woman of yours, that Y! She
    is rubbish, that woman of yours, her face is
    ugly, she smells like an evil spirit! Presently,
    when she is pregnant, I won't look after her!
You, B, you, her husband, you indeed, all by
    yourself, you can help her in childbirth!
All you others, eat . . .

Ah my daughter, my grandchild!
Ah, the snake with its tongue flickering, at
    Dagalbawei . . .
Ah, my daughter, ah, the mound of the snake!
Ah my grandchild! My grandchild!

At Bumbiwalwalyun, and far away, the snake
    scatters its young,
At Waidja and Dirmalangan, Ganal and Ngoiwul.
My daughter, my grandchild! My daughter is
    sick and hungry!
All you others, you eat till your bellies burst!
You used to be jealous before, when your
    husband called her.
All you lot are alive still—ah, my daughter, my
    grandchild!
Ah, your father has cried and cried, while mucus
    flowed into his mouth!
My daughter, my husband! My daughter, sick
    and hungry!
Ah, my daughter, my husband!
Presently your child will grow, and you won't be
    looking after him,
because you will be dead! Presently other
    children will hit him, other
women will not look after him properly . . . !
Ah, my daughter, my grandchild!

These songs come from North Eastern Arnhenland, Australia.

I am no longer afraid of death
I know well
Its dark and cold corridors
leading to life.

I am afraid rather of that life
which does not come out of death
which cramps our hands
and retards our march.

I am afraid of my fear
and even more of the fear of others,
who do not know where they are going,
who continue clinging
to what they consider to be life
which we know to be death!

Julia Esquivel

12

BLESSINGS

As the anonymous mother's blessing translated from the Gaelic shows, blessings, though they can be used in many different ways, are particularly moving as a parting prayer, a commending of another or of a group to safety, happiness, and good actions until those who part have the pleasure of meeting once more. Blessings leave a good taste on the palate, a sense of harmony and peace.

BLESSING

The blessing of God,
The eternal goodwill of God,
The shalom of God,
the wildness and the warmth of God,
be among us and between us
Now and always. Amen.

Anonymous

When people turn
from the table
where bread is broken
and candles glow,
be sure you have invited them
not to your house
but to their own,
and offered not your wisdom
but your love.

Anonymous

May the power and the mystery go before us, to
    show us the way,
shine above us to lighten our world,
lie beneath us to bear us up,

walk with us and give us companionship,

and glow and flow within us to bring us joy.
    Amen.

Judith Walker-Riggs

THE MOTHER'S BLESSING

Be the great God between thy two shoulders
To protect thee in thy going and in thy coming,
Be the Son of Mary Virgin near thine heart,
And be the perfect Spirit upon thee pouring—
Oh, the perfect Spirit upon thee pouring!

Gaelic, Anonymous

May the God who dances in creation,
and embraces us with human love,
who shakes our lives like thunder,
bless us and drive us out with power
to fill the world with her justice. Amen.

Janet Morley

About the Contributors

Alexander, Cecil Frances (1818–1895) An Irish poet and hymn-writer, she grew up in County Wicklow, Ireland. Her book *Hymns for Little Children* (1848) included three favorite hymns that are still widely sung today: "All Things Bright and Beautiful," "Once in Royal David's City," and "There Is a Green Hill Far Away." She also wrote Irish ballads. She was married to Bishop William Alexander.

Allshorn, Florence (1887–1950) A missionary in Uganda with the Church Missionary Society, she returned to Britain just before the Second World War with her health undermined. When she recovered, she set up the experiment of a lay community in Sussex, known as St. Julian's, which for forty years was a resource for people needing rest, a place of calm and beauty where they could recuperate and refind themselves.

She had original and practical insights about leading the spiritual life.

Austen, Jane (1775–1817) The daughter of a clergyman, she spent much of her life living in a rectory at Steventon, later at Chawton, both in the Hampshire countryside, in the south of England. Lack of money made it impossible for her to marry the man she loved. She was the author of *Pride and Prejudice* and other classic novels that placed her among the most famous of writers in the English language.

Bates, Katherine Lee (1859–1929) An American poet, she was born in Falmouth, Massachusetts, but spent much of her life in nearby Wellesley, where she became a professor of English at Wellesley College. She wrote or edited several scholarly books, but is most widely known as composer of the song "America the Beautiful."

Beatrijs of Nazareth (c.1200–c.1268) Beatrijs was born into a wealthy merchant family in the Brabant in Flanders, and was educated at first by the Beguines, then later by the Cistercians at Florival, where she received the same education a boy of the period would have had—the trivium and the quadrivium, a study of arts and sciences. She later learned calligraphy and manuscript illumination, and took vows as a

Cistercian nun. She became prioress of the convent of Our Lady of Nazareth at Lier. She was a scholar, writer, and poet, very much influenced, like some of her contemporaries, by the poetry of courtly love, which she applied to her relationship with God. Despite her skill in Latin, she chose to write in the Flemish dialect.

The Beguines This order of women was founded in the Netherlands in the twelfth century. They were a religious group and did not take vows; some lived in community, and some lived a lay life in their own homes. Their influence spread to other parts of northern Europe. They offered unique support and companionship to single women without insisting on the vows and austerities of convent life. They performed works of charity, which included caring for the sick and running schools. They included some fine women poets. They fell under papal disapproval at the Council of Vienne in 1311 when they, and their male counterparts, the Beghards, were accused of heresy and condemned. At least one Beguine was burned. Some of the women, like Mechthild of Magdeburg, joined convents for protection.

Bossis, Gabrielle (1874–1950) French author of *He and I*, a diary-style account of her discussions with Jesus.

Brontë, Anne (1820–1849) Born in Yorkshire, England, she was the youngest of the renowned Brontë literary family. Occasionally employed as governesses, she and her sisters Emily and Charlotte joined together in 1846 to pseudonymously publish *Poems* by *Currer, Ellis, and Acton Bell.* All three eventually publicly admitted their gender, continuing to write prolifically and publish some of the best-known novels and poems in the English language. Her two novels, *Agnes Grey* and *The Tenant of Wildfeld Hall* were published in 1847 and 1848, immediately before her death of tuberculosis in 1849.

Burgess, Ruth (1948–) She grew up in Birmingham, England, and South Wales and now lives in Sunderland, England. She is a member of the Iona Community, a Christian group attached to the island of Iona in western Scotland, who have produced some outstanding writing on Christian themes, in particular prayers and liturgical writing.

Carmichael, Amy (1867–1951) A Christian missionary in south India who wrote prolifically and well. She was an advocate for women and was especially concerned about the fate of children who were given to temples by their parents and sometimes neglected.

Clifton, Lucille (1936–) Born in Depew, New York, to a working class family of book lovers with no formal education, she attended Howard University as a drama major. An award-winning African-American poet of family history, relationships, community, and racial history, she has also published many books for children and young adults. Her published poems can be found in many books, including *Quilting: Poems 1987–1990* and *Good Woman: Poems and a Memoir: 1969–1980*. She has been the Distinguished Professor of Humanities at St. Mary's College of Maryland since 1991.

Coleridge, Mary (1861–1907) Born into a literary family in London, England, she was a descendant of Samuel Taylor Coleridge, and her parents entertained Tennyson, Browning, Ruskin, and several of the Pre-Raphaelite painters. She was a novelist, literary critic, and a rather shy poet, for a long time refusing to offer her poetry for publication.

Coolidge, Susan (1835–1905) Her real name was Sarah Chauncy Woolsey. She grew up in Cleveland, Ohio. She was the author of *What Katy Did* (1872) and two other much-loved Katy books, as well as other books for girls. Katy was a strong and rather rebellious heroine, which made her a novelty among the well-behaved children in many nineteenth-century children's books.

Cropper, Margaret (1886–1980) A poet who spent her life in Westmorland, England, she took much of her inspiration from its life and speech. Much of her poetry used Christian themes.

Dickinson, Emily (1830–1886) Born and lived all her life in Amherst, Massachusetts, she was educated at the Amherst Academy and Mount Holyoke Seminary. She lived as a recluse from the age of about thirty, and wrote over 2,000 poems, only seven of which were published in her lifetime. This was partly because of the advice of her mentor, Thomas Higginson, who, while recognizing her genius, felt that her work was too unconventional for publication. In 1890, however, Higginson and her Amherst friend Mabel Loomis Todd published a selection, which they called *Poems*. In 1960 a complete edition of her poems was published using the original typography and spellings, which her editors had changed.

Dobson, Rosemary (1920–) New South Wales, Australia-born poet. Winner of the Patrick White Award in 1984, her many books include her *Collected Poems* (1991).

Esquivel, Julia (1930–) An exile of her native Guatemala, she has spent much of her life working for the poor and the oppressed. Poet and theologian, she served on the staff of the World Council of Churches in Geneva. More recently, she taught at the Methodist Seminary in Mexico City, where she also worked with women's groups, Guatemalan refugees, the Jewish community, and international groups seeking justice for Latin America.

Falk, Marcia Born and raised in New York, she graduated from Brandeis University and Stanford University, where she earned a Ph.D. in English and comparative literature. She was a Fulbright Scholar in Bible and Hebrew literature at the Hebrew University in Jerusalem, eventually returning as a Postdoctoral Fellow. Along with writing her own poetry, she works to discover and translate old and new voices of other women poets, especially those writing in Hebrew and Yiddish. Her most recent work, *The Book of Blessings* (1997), is a prayer book that recreates Hebrew and English liturgy from a contemporary, nonhierarchical, gender-inclusive perspective. She is currently the Rabbi Sally Priesand Visiting Professor of Jewish Women's Studies at Hebrew Union College in Cincinnati.

Fuertes, Gloria (1918–1998) Born in Madrid into a poor family, she was the youngest of nine children and one of only three who survived childhood. She attended the Instituto de Educación Profesional de la Mujer, where she received the education that was then considered necessary for a future housewife. The Civil War and the loss of her fiancé changed her life, transforming her into a pacifist. In 1939 she wrote her first story for children. In 1950, her first poem, *Isla Ignorada*, was published, and she established *Versos con Faldas*, a group of female poets. A founder of *Arquero* magazine and a librarian at the International Institute of Madrid, she wrote many children's books and volumes of poetry. She received many awards for her work, including the Guipúzcoa Prize and the International Hans Christian Andersen award.

Foligno, Angela di (c.1248–c.1309) She was born of well-to-do parents in Umbria and married at twenty into a life of fashion and luxury. She was deeply influenced by St. Francis, and perhaps imitating the saint, she stood in front of the altar of the church of San Francesco and removed all her clothes as a sign of giving herself to God. Dramatically, her mother, husband, and children suddenly died—presumably in an epidemic—and Angela sold her country estate, gave away all her possessions, and joined the Third Order of Franciscans in order to care for lepers and the poor. It is not certain whether she could write, but her *Book of the Experience of the Truly Faithful,* which described thirty steps toward God, was dictated by her in the Umbrian dialect.

Gidlow, Elsa (1898–1986) She was one of the first openly lesbian writers in America and was indicted by

Senator Joseph McCarthy in the 1950s. She helped found the Druid Heights community in the California redwoods, of which Alan Watts and other writers and artists were members.

Gottlieb, Lynn (1949–) American, born in Bethlehem, Pennsylvania. She travelled to Israel as a high school exchange student and this experience kindled in her the desire to become a rabbi. There were no women rabbis at that time. Ordained in 1981, she is active in creating new, contemporary forms of Judaism, as reflected in her book, *She Who Dwells Within: A Feminist Vision of a Renewed Judaism* (1995). She once said: "God has a female presence but that presence is in exile. It is not until we redeem Her and bring Her home to rest in us that the entire world will be redeemed."

Greenberg, Florence (1882–1980) London-born cookery expert, journalist, and writer.

Griffiths, Ann (1776–1805) She grew up on a farm in Montgomeryshire, Wales, and had a deeply mystical temperament. She joined the Methodists in 1797. She married in 1804 and died the next year in childbirth. She was an outstandingly gifted writer of hymns, none of which were published until after her death.

Hadewijch of Brabant (mid-thirteenth century) An edu-cated woman who knew French and Latin but who chose to write in the Brabantine dialect, she used the tradition of the *minnesänger,* the poetry of courtly love, to write about her passion for God. She was a leader in the Beguine community, but for some unknown reason was disgraced.

Hare, Maria (1798–1870) British. She was a religious writer and diarist, who was born at Knutsford in Cheshire and educated mainly at home. She traveled widely in Europe and married the Reverend Augustus Hare. She designed an education program for home-bound mothers.

Hatshepsut, Queen of Egypt (1500 BCE) She was the daughter of Thutmose I and the half-sister of his suc-cessor, Thutmose II. When he died young, and his heir, Thutmose III, was still a child, Hatshepsut had herself made Pharaoh, a distinction unique for a woman, and ruled for many years before Thutmose III took his revenge and Hatshepsut disappeared. She built a magnificent temple at Deir el-Bahri near Thebes.

Havergal, Frances Ridley (1836–1879) A well-known British hymn-writer, she was born in Worcestershire, England, and educated at home. She published poetry, hymns, and a book called *Havergal's Psalmody,* and gave the proceeds to the Church Missionary Society. She refused all offers of marriage. She disapproved of women's rights and of "strong-minded women" in general.

Hildegard of Bingen (1098–1179) Born in the Rhineland, she was the tenth child in an aristocratic family and was given to her aunt Jutta, a hermit, at the age of eight, apparently as a form of tithing to show the devoutness of her family—a practice she was to deplore in her adult writing. She suffered acutely from appalling migraine headaches throughout her life. She took vows as a Benedictine nun at the age of fifteen. At the age of thirty-eight she followed her aunt as abbess of the monastery. She was multigifted as musician, poet, and biologist, and was deeply interested also in medicine. She had visions, many of which are detailed in her book *Scivias*. Toward the end of her life she embarked on preaching tours all over the countryside, an extraordinary project for a woman of her period.

Holtby, Winifred (1898–1935) She was born in Yorkshire, England, and had a deep love of the Yorkshire countryside, something very obvious in her novels, particularly in the most famous of them, *South Riding*. She served in France during the First World War as a WAAC, a member of the Women's Auxiliary Army Corps. She met the writer Vera Brittain at Oxford

University, and they shared a commitment to pacifism and to feminist principles. After Winifred Holtby's early death, Vera Brittain wrote a book about her: *Testament of Friendship* (1940).

Julian of Norwich (c.1342–c.1413) An English mystic, she lived as an anchoress outside the walls of St. Julian's Church, Norwich. (Unfortunately her cell was destroyed by bombing during the Second World War.) She received a series of visions on May 8, 1373, which she later wrote down, and these are known as *The Showings* or *Revelations of Divine Love.* Her theology placed a strong emphasis on the love of God—she believed that this would redeem all the souls in hell, an unusual and near-heretical belief at the time—and she used the image of mother love to illustrate the tenderness and forgiveness of God.

Lalleswari (fourteenth century) Born in Kashmir of an upper class Hindu family, she became a mystical poet. She left her husband and joined a sect called the Saivites, who believed that the human soul is one with God.

Levertov, Denise (1923–1997) She grew up in Ilford, Essex, and was educated at home by her Welsh mother and by her father, a Russian Jew, who settled in

England after the First World War and became an Anglican priest. She worked as a nurse in England but left for the United States in 1948 and lived in New York City. She had already published a volume of poetry in England. In America, under the mentorship of Kenneth Rexroth and later James Laughlin of New Directions, she was to publish much more poetry that would be greatly admired by literary critics and others. She was a very gifted poet, mystical yet down to earth. She campaigned for civil rights and against the Vietnam War, the Bomb, and U.S.-backed regimes in Latin America. She converted to Roman Catholicism.

Levy-Tanai, Sarah (1911–1975) A contemporary Israeli teacher and composer of children's songs, she was born in Jerusalem to Yemenite parents and then orphaned at a young age. Her song compositions include the popular "Kol Dodi" (My Love's Voice). In 1949, she founded the Inbal Dance Troupe and in 1973 she received the Israel Prize for her contribution to dance in Israel.

Lewin, Ann (1936–) She lives in Southampton, Hampshire, England. She worked for twenty-seven years as a teacher, and then as a student welfare adviser at Southampton University. She writes poetry and prayers. Her latest volume of poetry is *Candles and Kingfishers* (2000). She gives retreats and quiet days.

Mechthild of Magdeburg (c.1210–1280) Born into a noble Saxon family, at fifteen she joined the Beguines and remained a member for forty years. She was a mystic and spiritual writer and wrote *The Flowing Light of the Godhead.* Like other Beguines, she was interested in the poetry of courtly love. In old age she joined the Cistercian convent at Helfta, possibly as protection from the Inquisition.

Markova, Dawna Internationally known for her ground-breaking work in helping people learn with passion and live on purpose. She is the CEO of Professional Thinking Partners, Inc., in Utah, co-founder of the Worldwide Women's Web, and former research affili-ate of the Organizational Learning Center at Massachusetts Institute of Technology. Her books include *I Will Not Die an Unlived Life, The Open Mind,* and *No Enemies Within; An Unused Intelligence,* co-authored with her husband and business partner, Andy Bryner; and *How Your Child Is Smart* and *Learning Unlimited,* co-authored with Anne R. Powell. She also co-edited *Random Acts of Kindness,* has been a frequent guest on National Public Radio, and was featured on a PBS special.

McIlhagga, Kate (1938–) She grew up in Glasgow, Scotland, and would have liked to have been ordained in the Church of Scotland when she left the University of St. Andrew's in the 1960s, but women could not be ordained in the Church of Scotland at the time, so she trained as a youth and community worker. She married and had three sons. In 1981 she was ordained as a United Reformed minister, and in the same year she became a member of the Iona Community. At present she is a minister of three rural parishes in North Northumberland and is beginning to prepare for retirement.

Meynell, Alice (1847–1922) Born of a well-to-do and artistic family in London, she spent her childhood mostly in Italy and Switzerland where she was privately educated by her father. She converted to Roman Catholicism in 1872. In 1875 she published a volume of poetry, *Preludes,* which was much admired by Ruskin, W. M. Rossetti and George Eliot. She married the distinguished journalist and editor Wilfred Meynell, and they co-edited a number of journals. She was a supporter of women's suffrage, and was concerned about the social status of women. She disliked sentimental mentions of "the feminine," saying that it was a force, not a grace.

Mirabai (c.1498–c.1550) She was born in Rajasthan and raised as a princess. She was married at eighteen to the Rajput heir apparent but was widowed before he ascended the throne. Mirabai, who all her life had a devotion to Krishna, gave herself up to religious practices and left the court for a series of journeys. She was an adept of the medieval yogic tradition of the north of India, a *bhakta* — a devoted one — searching for and submitting to the supreme reality, Krishna. Aesthetics and enlightenment were combined in this tradition, and Mirabai was an accomplished musician and sang her compositions.

Morley, Janet (1951–) She wrote some of the first inclusive prayers used in Britain, which were then widely used and admired both for their use of language and for their theological excellence. She went on to work as adult education adviser for Christian Aid, where she continued to write and edit material for use by Christian groups. She is now working for the Methodist Church as secretary for adult learning.

Oodgeroo of the Noonuccal (Kath Walker) (1920–1993) A well-known Australian poet from the Noonuccal tribe of Stradbroke Island, near Brisbane, she reverted to her tribal name as a protest against the bicentennial celebrations of 1988. She has published several books of poetry. Under the name of Kath Walker she had been made a Member of the British Empire in 1971.

Rabi'a the Mystic (ninth century) A Sufi saint born of poor parents in Basra and orphaned as a child, she was sold into slavery but later freed. She devoted much of her life to prayer.

Ratushinskaya, Irina (1954–) Born in Russia, she was arrested in Kiev at the age of twenty-eight and sentenced to seven years hard labor and five years internal exile, accused of anti-Soviet agitation and propaganda, on account of her poetry. In a labor camp in Mordovia, she was held in a special unit for women political prisoners where she suffered beatings, force-feeding, and solitary confinement at temperatures so cold that the KGB told her she would never be able to bear children. She continued to write poetry in the prison, and the poems were smuggled out and published, arousing interest in her plight around the world. In 1986, on the eve of the Reykjavik summit, she was released. She came to London and eventually settled with her husband in Britain, where six years later she gave birth to twin sons. She has continued to write.

Riccuiti, Gail Reverend and Associate Professor of Homiletics, Colgate Rochester Divinity School, she has served churches in Massillon, Ohio, and in Byron and Rochester, New York, and she was Vice Moderator of the 189th General Assembly (UPCUSA). She is co-author of the two-volume *Birthings and Blessings*.

Ridler, Anne (1912–) She grew up in Warwickshire, England, and was educated at King's College, London. She worked as secretary and editorial assistant to T.S. Eliot, and later in publishing. She married and had four children. She wrote poetry, plays, and an opera libretto; made translations of opera libretti; and edited several well-known poets.

Rossetti, Christina (1830–1894) She lived in London, where she was closely associated with the group of religious painters known as the Pre-Raphaelite Brotherhood, of which her brother, Dante Gabriel Rossetti, was a member. She was a poet and the author of many poems on themes of love or religion, as well as the longer, very sensual poem "Goblin Market."

St. Bridget of Kildare (fifth century) Irish holy woman. She is often called St. Brigid, St. Bride, or St. Bridget of Kildare. Little is known about her, but she did found a great monastery at Kildare. She is buried at Downpatrick with St. Patrick and St. Columba, and with them she is patron of Ireland; hence her nickname Mary of the Gael. St. Bridget is associated notably with charity and justice. Devotion to her was widespread in Great Britain before the Protestant Reformation, as witnessed in many names, e.g., Bridewell, Kilbride, Kirkbride, and McBride. Her Feast Day is celebrated February 1.

St. Hilda Community This community, founded in 1987, is a prayer group of women and men, which began meeting in the East End of London, at first as a form of protest at the Church of England's refusal to allow women ordained in other countries to celebrate Holy Communion in its churches. The Community openly invited visiting women priests to celebrate in the university chapel where they held their meetings, from which the Community was eventually expelled on the orders of the then Bishop of London. (This was at a time when the Church of England was still undecided about whether to ordain women.) The group wrote many prayers and liturgies using inclusive language, and went on to publish two books of prayers: *Women Included* (1991) and *New Women Included* (1996). The Community still meets regularly.

Sappho (c. 610–c. 580 BCE) She was born on Lesbos but later lived at Mytilene, though for a while she was exiled from there to Sicily. Only two complete examples of her odes remain, though there are beautiful fragments of other poems. Her use of the four-line stanza, which Catullus and Horace went on to use, gave the name *Sapphic* to this literary form. Because Sappho wrote with admiration and affection of a group of women and girls to whom she seems to have been a leader, or possibly teacher, the island Lesbos has given the word *lesbian* for women who are sexually attracted to other women. It is not known whether Sappho herself actually was lesbian. She married and had a daughter, Cleis.

Shakers Popular name for the Millennial Church, an eighteenth-century body, which, because of persecution in England, left for America in 1774. They settled near Albany, New York, and later had other settlements in different parts of the country. They were led by Mother Ann Lee, whom they regarded as the "female principle in Christ" as Jesus had been the "male principle." They practiced celibacy and renewed their numbers by conversion. They were famous for their music and dancing and for the simple beauty of the furniture, houses, and farm implements that they made.

Shemer, Naomi (1931–) Israeli composer, known as "the First Lady of Israeli Song." Her popular songs include "Yerushalayim shel Zahav" (Jerusalem of Gold) and "Lu Yehi" (Let It Be), which was inspired by The

Beatles' tune of the same name. She won the Israel Prize in 1983.

Shepperson, Janet She is a member of the Corrymeela Community in Northern Ireland and wrote *The Furthest North You Can Go.*

Sholl, Betsy Winner of the 1997 Felix Pollak Prize in Poetry for her fifth book of poetry *Don't Explain,* she grew up on the New Jersey shore and holds degrees from Bucknell University, the University of Rochester, and Vermont College. She has published five books of poetry, including *Changing Faces, Appalachian Winter,* and *Rooms Overhead.* The fourth, *The Red Line,* won the 1991 Associated Writing Programs Award for Poetry. She teaches at the University of Southern Maine and at Vermont College.

Starhawk (1951–) American, she is one of the primary voices of the ecofeminism and Goddess movements. She is the author or coauthor of eight books, including *The Spiral Dance* and *The Twelve Wild Swans* (2000).

Sumner, Mary (1828–1921) As the wife of the Rector of Old Alresford in Hampshire, she felt a need to bring together country women of different backgrounds — "cottage women and elegant and aristocratic women," as she put it—in the common enterprise of giving their children a spiritual upbringing. She founded the Mothers' Union in 1876, an Anglican organization, which now has 750,000 members concerned with the well-being of families worldwide.

St. Teresa of Ávila (1515–1582) She entered a Carmelite convent as a young woman, but it was very casually run, with the nuns entertaining young men from the town. After some years of boredom and discontent and an unexplained severe illness, Teresa underwent a spiritual change. She began to pray at great depth and to have unusual spiritual experiences of levitation and ecstasy. She was later to found her own stricter form of the Carmelite life, the Discalced (i.e., without shoes) Carmelites, and set up houses for friars and nuns all over Spain. She was a friend of St. John of the Cross. She wrote what was almost a scientific study of the stages of prayer, and combined mystical experiences with an extremely busy and practical life.

Teresa, Mother (1910–1997) Born in Yugoslavia, of Albanian parents, she grew up in Macedonia. She went to India in 1928 to join an order of nuns, the Sisters of Loretto, and she taught in their school and eventually became the headmistress of it. In 1948, however, she felt a call to work in the slums of Calcutta, and by 1950 she had started her own order, the Order of the Missionaries of Charity. In 1952 she established the House for the Dying, where her work became famous. It spread widely both in India and in other parts of the world. She was awarded the Nobel Peace Prize in 1979.

St. Thérèse of Lisieux (1873–1897) Born in a deeply devout family, Thérèse followed her two older sisters into the Carmelite convent in Lisieux at the age of fifteen. A spoiled child at home, she suffered a good deal under a harsh superior. She worked out what she called her "Little Way," a spiritual method in which whatever happened could be accepted as a way of loving God, described by her in her moving autobiography *The History of a Soul.* She died of tuberculosis at the age of twenty-four. She was much loved and admired in France, and many village churches there still have statues of Thérèse. During the First World War, many French soldiers went into battle carrying medallions of Thérèse. She was canonized in 1925.

Therigata nuns (c.500–400 BC) These were female disciples of the Buddha (their male equivalent were known as Theragata) who had given up worldly preoccupations to live a nomadic and contemplative life with minimal possessions in the forests and parks of India. *Therigata* means "songs of the nuns." They were accomplished poets, encouraged by the Buddha to use local dialect in their poem/prayers, rather than the formal scholarly language of Sanskrit.

Underhill, Evelyn (1875–1941) She came from a well-to-do background and was privately educated before taking her degree at King's College, London. She taught the philosophy of religion for a while at Manchester College, Oxford. She married Hubert Stuart Moore and lived for many years in Campden Hill Square in London. She was interested in mystical experience and wrote a classic book about it: *Mysticism* (1911). She underwent a conversion experience and became an Anglican. She was very much influenced by the Catholic theologian Friedrich von Hugel (1852–1925), but she never became a Catholic. She continued to write and became well-known as a giver of retreats and as a spiritual director, which was unusual for women in the early twentieth century.

Waddell, Helen (1889–1965) Of Irish descent, she was born in Tokyo, of a Presbyterian missionary and Chinese scholar, Hugh Waddell. She returned to Ireland to go to school and university in Belfast where her studies in

Latin later helped with her translations of medieval Latin poetry. Her books about the Middle Ages introduced many readers to the period. Her novel about the medieval Scholastic Peter Abelard, *Peter Abelard* (1933), was a huge success, selling thirty editions. She also published some translations from the Chinese.

Walker, Alice (1944–) American novelist from Georgia. She studied at Sarah Lawrence College, and went on to work as teacher and social worker in New York City. She was active in the Civil Rights movement. *The Color Purple* (1982) won the Pulitzer Prize, and was made into a film by Steven Spielberg.

Walker, Kath (See Oodgeroo of the Noonuccal)

Walker-Riggs, Judith American, she is currently Interim Minister of the Main Line Unitarian Church in Devon, Pennsylvania. She earned a Doctor of Divinity degree from Meadville/Lombard Theological School in Chicago, and is a frequent guest speaker and preacher.

Waring, Anna Laetitia (1823–1910) Born in Glamorgan, Wales, and brought up as a Quaker, she converted to Anglicanism in 1842 and became a well-known hymn writer. Her *Hymns and Meditations* (1850) went into twenty editions. In addition to writing, she was a constant visitor to Bristol prison and worked for the Prisoners' Aid Society. She never married, but lived with her three sisters.

Watt, Jean Macdonald (1915–) Born in Reading, England, of Scottish and Welsh parentage, she has lived in Scotland since 1933. She is a mother and grandmother, and has been a social worker. Her interests are music, painting, and writing. She has published poetry and prose translations from French and German.

Weil, Simone (1909–1943) A Parisian, Simone Weil was a contemporary of Simone de Beauvoir and Jean-Paul Sartre at the Ecole Normale Supérieure. She taught philosophy but also worked in the Renault car factory as a way of sharing the life of the working class. She went to Spain to serve in the Civil War but was soon invalided home after an accident. She was attracted by Christianity but repelled by the way it was practiced. She wrote several books on religious themes and had a strong mystical sense. She died in an English hospital during the Second World War, partly of tuberculosis, partly from starving herself so as not to eat more than her contemporaries under the Nazi occupation of France.

Winter, Miriam Thérèse Medical Mission Sister and Professor of Liturgy, Worship, Spirituality, and Feminist Studies at Hartford Seminary, Hartford, Connecticut, she is also a musician and writer. She has worked with the hungry and the homeless on four continents. Her many books include *The Singer and the Song* (a memoir), *WomanWisdom*, and *The Gospel According to Mary*. She earned a Ph.D. in Liturgical Studies at Princeton Theological Seminary.

Wright, Judith (1915–2000) An Australian from Armidale, New South Wales, born into a prominent farming family, she had a distinguished literary career as a poet, publishing eleven books of poetry. She also worked on issues of human rights, conservation and Aboriginal land rights.

I regret that there are some women whose works are included in this collection whose life and work, despite research, I still know very little about. If they or their friends read this book, I would be glad to learn more.   —M. F.

Credits

The author is grateful to the following authors and publishers for permission to reproduce the material listed below. This page constitutes a continuation of the copyright page.

The late Florence Allshorn and the St. Julian's Trust, Coolham, Sussex, England, for excerpts from *The Notebooks of Florence Allshorn* selected and arranged by a member of St. Julian's Community. Published by St. Julian's, 1990.

National Aboriginal and Torres Strait Islander Catholic Council, Australia, for "Aboriginal Jubilee Prayer."

SPCK for the poem by Beatrijs of Nazareth from *Beguine Spirituality: An Anthology* by Fiona Bowie. Translations by Oliver Davies (London: SPCK, 1989).

Gabrielle Bossis and Brother Steven Prizzo of Librairie Mediaspaul of Sherbrooke, Quebec, Canada, for quotations from *He and I* (Editions Paulines).

Ruth Burgess for *The Desert*.

E. Richard Brodhag for "Think through Me" and "It Is Not Far to Go" by Amy Carmichael from *Mountain Breezes*, published by CLC Books, Fort Washington, Pa.

SPCK for *Harvest Prayer* by Lilian Cox from *Little Book of Prayers* (London: SPCK, 1988).

Curtis Brown Pty. Ltd., Sydney, Australia, for "The Edge" and "Folding the Sheets" by Rosemary Dobson.

Julia Esquivel for "I Am No Longer Afraid of Death."

Hardie St. Martin for "Bird's Nest" by Gloria Fuertes.

Monica Furlong for "In This Good World" from *God's a Good Man* (London: Mowbray, 1974).

Celeste West and Booklegger Publishing, P.O. Box 460654, San Francisco, CA 94146, (415) 642-7569, for Elsa Gidlow's work.

Lynn Gottlieb and HarperCollins for "Greeting Shekinah" from *She Who Dwells Within*, © 1995 by Lynn Gottieb. Reprinted with permission.

Hamlyn Publishers for the charoseth recipe from *Jewish Cookery* by Florence Greenberg (London: Hamlyn, 1958.).

SPCK for the poem by Hadewijch of Brabant from *Beguine Spirituality: An Anthology* by Fiona Bowie. Translations by Oliver Davies (London: SPCK, 1989).

Cool Grove Press, Brooklyn, New York, for poems from *Sweet on My Lips: The Love Poems of Mirabai*. Translated by Louise Landes Levi and P. Tej Hazeinika.

Janet Morley and SPCK for "Ash Wednesday Prayer" and "May the God who dances in creation" from *All Desires Known* (London: SPCK, 1989).

SPCK for the prayer by Mother Teresa from *The Silence of the Heart* edited by Kathryn Spink (London: SPCK, 1989).

John Wiley & Sons Australia for "Song" and "We Are Going" by Oodgeroo of the tribe Noonuccal (formerly known as Kath Walker) from *My People*, third edition (Jacaranda Press, 1990). Reprinted by permission of John Wiley & Sons Australia.

Andrew Nurnberg Associates, London, for poems by Irina Ratushinskaya from *Dance with a Shadow* translated by David McDuff (Newcastle, England: Bloodaxe Books, 1992).

Carcanet Press for "Choosing a Name" by Anne Ridler from *Collected Poems* (Manchester, England: Carcanet Press, 1988).

The St. Hilda Community, London, and SPCK for "We adore," "We stand at the turning of the year," and "We hold up our smallness to your greatness" from *Women Included* (London: SPCK, 1991).

Betsy Sholl for an excerpt from "Job's Wife" from *Rooms Overhead*, Alice James Books (Farmington, Maine: Alice James Books, 1986).

SPCK for the prayer by Thérèse of Lisieux from *The SPCK Book of Christian Prayer* (London: SPCK, 1995).

Shambhala Publications, Inc., for poems of the Therigata nuns from *Songs of the Sons and Daughters of the Buddha*, translated by Andrew

Index of First Lines

9 781683 365129